The Disobedient Museum

T0383714

The Disobedient Museum: Writing at the Edge aims to motivate disciplinary thinking to reimagine writing about museums as an activity where resistant forms of thinking, seeing, feeling, and acting can be produced and theorized as a form of protest against disciplinary stagnation.

Drawing on a range of cultural, theoretical, and political approaches, Kylie Message examines links between methods of critique today and moments of historical and disciplinary crisis, and asks what contribution museums might make to these, either as direct actors or through activities that sit more comfortably within their institutional remit. Identifying the process of writing about museums as a form of activism that brings together and elaborates on cultural and political agendas for change, the book explores how a process of engaged critique might benefit museum studies, what this critique might look like, and how museum studies might make a contribution to discourses of social and political change.

The Disobedient Museum is the first volume in Routledge's innovative Museums in Focus series and will be of great interest to scholars and students in the fields of museum studies, heritage studies, public history, and cultural studies. It should also be essential reading for museum practitioners, particularly those engaged with questions about the role of museums in regard to social activism and contentious contemporary challenges.

Kylie Message is Associate Professor and Senior Fellow in the Humanities Research Centre at the Australian National University. She is the Series Editor of 'Museums in Focus'.

Routledge Museums in Focus
Series Editor: Kylie Message

Committed to the articulation of big, even risky, ideas in small format publications, Museums in Focus challenges authors and readers to experiment
with, innovate, and press museums and the intellectual frameworks through
which we view these. It encourages debate about the cultural value and
political nature of museums and heritage in contemporary society, and wel-
comes attempts to radically rethink the way we engage with museums in
intellectual life to better articulate the relationship between culture, politics, and academic scholarship about museums and related cultural products
and phenomena. The series offers a platform for approaches that radically
rethink the relationships between cultural and intellectual dissent and crisis
and debates about museums, politics and the broader public sphere.

Recently published titles:

The Disobedient Museum
Writing at the Edge
Kylie Message

www.routledge.com/Museums-in-Focus/book-series/MIF

⌐MUSEUMS IN FOCUS⌐

Logo by James Verdon (2017).

The Disobedient Museum
Writing at the Edge

Kylie Message

Routledge
Taylor & Francis Group

LONDON AND NEW YORK

First published 2018 by Routledge

2 Park Square, Milton Park, Abingdon, Oxfordshire OX14 4RN
52 Vanderbilt Avenue, New York, NY 10017

Routledge is an imprint of the Taylor & Francis Group, an informa business

First issued in paperback 2019

British Library Cataloguing-in-Publication Data
A catalogue record for this book is available from the British Library

Library of Congress Cataloging-in-Publication Data
A catalog record for this title has been requested

ISBN: 978-1-138-24011-7 (hbk)
ISBN: 978-0-367-88619-6 (pbk)

Typeset in Times New Roman
by Apex CoVantage, LLC

REBELMUSE_ROUTLEDGE

Image by James Verdon (2017).

#THEDISOBEDIENTMUSEUM
@REBELMUSE_ROUTLEDGE

Logo by James Verdon (2017).

For Oscar and Ezra

Contents

List of illustrations

Series preface

Museums in Focus is a series of short format books published by Routledge that aims to foster debate about the cultural value and political nature of museums and heritage in contemporary society. It encourages attempts to radically rethink the way we engage with museums in intellectual life to better articulate the relationship of culture, politics, and academic scholarship about museums to related cultural products and phenomena.

Committed to the articulation of big, even risky ideas in small format publications, the series challenges authors and readers to experiment with, innovate, and press museums and the intellectual frameworks through which we view these in order to keep exploring, questioning, and extending knowledge in the fields of museum studies, heritage and cultural studies, and cognate fields such as history, art history, anthropology, and archaeology to find new ways of transferring knowledge with others in, beyond, and outside related fields.

The intellectual hypothesis motivating the series is that museums are not innately 'useful', 'safe', or even 'public' places, and that recalibrating our thinking about them might benefit from adopting a more radical and transgressive form of logic and approach. Examining this problem requires a level of comfort with (or at least tolerance of) ideas of crisis, dissent, protest, and radical thinking, and authors might benefit from considering how cultural and intellectual crisis, regeneration, and anxiety have been approached in other disciplines and contexts. The challenge requires brave and committed scholarship, as well as debate between and across diverse disciplinary and theoretical/practical contexts in order to force a constant process of intellectual reflection and questioning of the museological canon as it currently stands.

Acknowledgments

The writing of this book coincided with and is, as such, a product of a difficult and extended period of crisis. Despite its short length, it would almost certainly not exist without the help and support of family, friends, colleagues, and students, and without Routledge's unfettered enthusiasm for the Museums in Focus initiative. I am very thankful to the editorial team at Routledge for their support, advice, and professionalism. I have also been overwhelmed by the extent of interest I have received in the series thus far by readers and contributors, and I am very excited to see what directions forthcoming titles will lead the series in.

I am grateful to all those who have made intellectual contributions to the work presented here, including referees of the initial proposal, and Conal McCarthy and Richard Sandell who made particularly productive and insightful comments on the draft manuscript. Any shortcomings with content, logic, argumentation, or intellectual positioning are, however, my sole responsibility. I have benefitted from ongoing institutional support provided by the Research School of Humanities and the Arts, and the College of Arts and Social Sciences at the Australian National University. I am indebted to my colleagues – Paul Pickering, Kate Bowan, Toni Makkai, Ann Evans, and Andrea Witcomb from Deakin University – for their ongoing support and friendship. I am exceptionally grateful to James Verdon for designing *The Disobedient Museum* and *Museums in Focus* logos that appear in the front section of the book and in other places.

Research around the rallies described in Chapter 1 occurred during my time as a Smithsonian Research Fellow, and I continue to be grateful for the opportunities and funding provided to me by the Division of Political History at the National Museum of American History. This research was also supported by the Australian Government through the Australian Research Council's *Discovery Projects* funding scheme (project ID: DP0984602). I also acknowledge *Museum and Society*, in which a section of Chapter 3 was previously published (Message 2009a). Intellectually, this book has taken me on many journeys and has given me reason to revisit some cherished work by scholars, including Greg Dening, whom I had the pleasure of meeting as a PhD student and whose ideas are explored in Chapter 3. Ewan Johnston and Bob and Jill Message have each played important parts in that journey, and I continue to be indebted to them for their ongoing support. Finally, I am particularly grateful to Guy Jones. For him, only all the words and yet none of the words will do. And my children, who have, at times, excelled as role models in the arts of disobedience but who have, in so doing, offered a constant reminder to me of Greg Dening's advice in his 2004 book *Beach Crossings* about the importance to '[d]are to voyage across times, cultures, and self. Especially self'. Thanks, O and E; keep daring to cross boundaries. This book is for you.

This is not a protest. This is a process[1]

Figure 0.1 Preparations and staging tests the day before the Restoring Honor rally on the National Mall, Washington, D.C., August 27, 2010

Photograph by Kylie Message.

This is a book about writing about museums. My primary case study is the process of writing, and my subject matter consists of forms of critique. My frameworks for critical engagement are drawn from the interdisciplinary fields of museum studies, cultural studies, contemporary art theory, and cognate disciplines including sociology, anthropology, and history. My intention is to explore and make a case for the potential that disciplinary- and interdisciplinary-based modes of critique (and engagements with perceptions of crisis) have in making a political impact, recognizing that such an outcome takes a variety of formal/public, as well as informal/'behind-the-scenes' approaches. So to be precise, this book is both a political statement (protest) and a process, and it takes as its starting point the premise that these terms are deeply interconnected.

The book has two main aims. The first is to argue that studies of culture generally and studies of museums specifically can make a significant contribution to understandings about social protest and reform movements.[2] The second is to argue that writing about museums can itself be a form of intellectual activism that has the potential to impact on museums and the sociopolitical context in which museums operate. Based on research into museums, political activism, and discourses of critical engagement, this book starts from the understanding that museums are not innately 'useful', 'safe', or even 'public' places, and contends that recalibrating our thinking about them requires a level of comfort (if not direct engagement) with ideas of crisis, dissent, protest, and radical thinking. It offers a preliminary overview of the relationship between academic theory and activist culture in museum and sociopolitical contexts to establish pathways for investigating connections between crisis and regeneration in disciplinary contexts in order to ask whether (and how) museums have contributed to the activity of agenda setting for debates over cultural crisis, as well as what role writing about museums might have for progressing social justice aims.

The intellectual premise of the book is that the interdisciplinary field of museum studies functions as a kind of boundary discipline, meaning that it occupies the conceptual spaces that are typically assumed to exist 'in-between' traditional disciplinary canons (such as history and anthropology), dichtomized terms (such as theory and practice), and the spaces of conflict between territories or positions defined in opposition to each other (such as the political 'left' versus the political 'right'). Rather than being narrowly contained within these border zones, the interdisciplinary work that is done in these spaces is expansive and transgresses the edges of the disciplines, terms and territories that it rubs against. It is both influenced by and infiltrates its neighboring fields to show the relationships that exist across normative disciplinary distinctions. The book models a 'disobedient' framework for challenging the normativity of traditional disciplinary approaches to knowledge formation. It advocates a form of engaged research that draws on a foundation of historical practices, as well as disciplinary forms of critique to investigate the politics of museums and ultimately challenge museum studies about the ways it has typically addressed the connections between culture and politics.

While this book draws on interdisciplinary approaches to map the conceptual terrain of the disobedient museum, it is not a book about disciplinarity per se.[3] Yet as I have already indicated and as will become a core theme throughout the book, interdisciplinarity relies on a complex network of relationships – oftentimes awkward – with practices and traditions of disciplinary thinking. Despite the prima facie connotations with modern forms of rationality and instrumentalized forms of knowledge production and legitimation associated with institutions such as museums and universities (Best and Kellner 1991),[4] I have elected to retain use of the term 'disciplinarity' as a way to keep these networks apparent, to keep calling the field's constituent terms and relations into question, as a way of encouraging the terms to 'interrogate each other, to negotiate the boundaries between them' (Mitchell 1995: 543). Instead of looking for a 'post-disciplinary' or 'post-critical' framework that might be associated with post- or hypermodernity (see Prior 2003: 52, 69 fn 2), I have kept the term in play as a tactic to keep the limitations of the concept of disciplinarity in our line of vision. It is one way of signaling how the limits of discursive legibility can provide a space of risk in which new or reconstituted assemblages of meaning are generated.[5]

I have identified spaces of disciplinary risk (where recuperation into mainstream narratives or modernist paradigms are as much a possible outcome as the collapse of meaning) as the worksite of the disobedient museum in order to illuminate how disciplines interact comfortably as well as with dissonance to produce what visual culture theorist W.J.T. Mitchell calls spaces of 'indiscipline' (Mitchell 1995: 541).[6] My tactical use of disciplinarity has developed partly in response to the politically engaged (if not active) work of, at, and by many contemporary museums. This engagement aims to provide a pathway for greater interaction between constituent terms than that allowed by what Nick Prior (2003: 51) disparagingly calls the 'orthodoxy in academic writings on postmodern culture' that appear determined to 'record the death rattle of the project of the museum as it was forged in the crucible of European Enlightenment'. What is needed, according to Prior, espousing a view I share, is 'an approach that treats "strong" forms of postmodern theorizing with caution, but remains equally skeptical of static conceptions of the museum as unchanged since the nineteenth century' (Prior 2006: 520; also Message 2006).[7]

My 'disobedient' approach centralizes disciplinary borderwork/border transgression as a methodology for interdisciplinarity and engaged research. This approach is a conceptual one that I present here as a model for others interested in engaging with urgent critical problems involving museums, politics, and society.[8] Rather than being prescriptive, it offers one possible way of recalibrating museum studies to highlight the importance of methodological clarity, engaged research work, and intellectual rigor for the practice of writing about museums. I have used the term 'disobedient museum' to describe this process of intellectual activism for two reasons. First, to disrupt traditional definitions and understandings associated with the traditional/canonistic terms of 'museum' and 'museology' (Desvallées and Mairesse 2009) and, second, to demonstrate the analogies and connections that exist between politically engaged museum work and politically engaged writing about museums (extending the approach taken in Message 2014; Message 2015; Message and Witcomb 2015). Finally, the term is meant to challenge and extend traditional understandings of museums by arguing that the process of writing about museum politics is similar to many of the processes of meaning construction that museums undertake.

The book's attention to conceptual and disciplinary boundaries also aims to provoke discussion about the 'museum-like' spaces and activities that exist outside of or on the edges of formal museum spaces. An institutional example of a museum-like event is the annual Smithsonian Folklife Festival. An example of an informal museum-like event is the January 2017, Women's March on Washington that took place on the National Mall, a location that Lonnie Bunch, Director of the National Museum of African American History and Culture, has called 'America's front lawn' (quoted in Cunningham 2016). Regardless of whether they are formal or informal and of the particular agenda they advocate (a pro-life or pro-gun rally on the Mall would also offer an informal example), these activities embody a form of cultural politics and are considered 'disobedient' because they are located at boundary sites or edges and simultaneously work across these borders, which are as much epistemic and structural as they are imaginary. Addressing diverse and heterogeneous audiences, these activities seek to produce sites that generate responses or exchanges that are positive, negative, or both. Rather than conforming with traditional museum definitions, the disobedient museum project is more closely aligned with the activities and agendas that I have described as being museum-like. The disobedient museum does not seek to progress an 'anti-museum' stance, and it does not offer a straightforward rejection of forms of governance, discourse, or disciplinarity but instead is a project space that identifies institutional edges as potential sites of affective action. The disobedient museum project is ultimately a form of intellectual activism that takes a variety of forms and outcomes (including writing, museums, rallies, marches, and other forms of political protest) to emphasize *processes* of borderwork that seek to transgress traditional disciplinary models and highlight new connections or reframe existing or new sites of conflict.

This book typically uses the disobedient museum concept to refer to a process or site of writing that emphasizes interconnections with processes used by museum activists, political protest and reform movements, and intellectual activism around practices of critique and self-reflexivity. It also aims to articulate the contributions that each of these three areas makes to the others. What impact does museum work have on public forms of protest? What influence does a critically reflective and engaged form of writing have on museum work? What are the collaborations that occur across these three fields of action? As these questions (which are representative rather than exhaustive) indicate, the disobedient museum is a process that is expansive. And while this book touches on each of these three areas – Chapter 1 analyzes political protest, Chapter 2 interprets the effects of disciplinary crisis in this context, and Chapter 3 recommends modes for writing resistance – it is beyond the scope of the book to investigate the questions fully or to thoroughly examine the intersections that exist across each area. In the final instance, my overriding aim is to introduce the disobedient museum as a concept and an approach for thinking about how to write about museums. Subsequent publications in this series expand on this framework to explore the other areas in relation to case studies focused on specific interactions between museums and political actions, events, and protest (forthcoming titles include *Museums and Racism* and *Curatorial Activism*).

The book emphasizes frames of reference associated with critical theory (and social movement studies derived from sociology; also see Message 2015) in order to explore diverse approaches to understanding the relationships between collective action, contention, and museums in relation to public institutions that play a role in building and representing collective identity in the form of nationhood or other shared ideas of belonging. This approach has developed from my motivation to better understand the interactions between social structure – the macro and enduring set of (usually) orderly relationships between defining categories such as class, race, and ethnicity – and the more pragmatic institutional or governmental structures that regulate public policy making and guide museum procedures. In this context, the collective protest and reform movements that seek to challenge broader social structures impact on and are also influenced by institutional change and transformation. Disciplinary approaches toward analyzing this relationship are typically constrained by their own discourses and methodologies such that social movement theory, for example, has been criticized for its reticence to engage with cultural (and to an extent qualitative) elements of protest and for its inability to develop theoretical frameworks and forms of analysis relevant to activists and the causes they represent (Haenfler, Johnson, and Jones 2012; Message 2015: 253; Polletta 1997; Snow 2004). What has rarely been asked, from any singular disciplinary position, is what impact museums' (often behind-the-scenes) actions may have on progressing or supporting political change. An exception is a recent review of the National Museum of African American History and Culture by Steven W. Thrasher (2016), who asks, '[I]f the Oval Office can't help our cause, can a museum?'[9]

While it is true that not all museums (or museum writers) have explicitly political agendas, museums and writing about museums are never, regardless of intentions, benign or politically neutral activities. I have focused in this book on connections between museums, writing, and social/political change because I see museum work and writing about museums as activities that are aligned to intellectual activism and that have the potential to make a greater contribution to political discourse and action than has perhaps been previously recognized. This potential is specifically related to the ability of museums and writing to occupy and explore edges that are disciplinary as well as social and political. While I agree for the most part with Thrasher's criticism that museums cannot easily act as explicitly political instruments (regardless of how *politicized* they may be), in some cases they can and do function as a bridge between 'the people' and their government to progress or facilitate change (as per the case studies in Message 2014). Where they do provide such an interface, it often results from a direct engagement (often 'behind-the-scenes') with protest and reform movements or by emphasizing relationships between political culture and cultures of political work and intervention within a space that is typically associated with structural conditions of power. Whether these actions are interpreted as a form of subversion against structural conditions or as the recuperation of forms of resistance is probably more subjective than measurable; however, in having the same expectations of museums and the Oval Office, Thrasher (2016) starts from the premise that museums are spaces that are potentially politically affective.

My interest in exploring the capacity of culture to act on politics has grown out of research and analysis conducted by others working across the fields of research in which I work. A specific influence has, of course, been museum studies, which has increasingly articulated a requirement that museums should not just be politically aware but actively and demonstrably engaged with political change, particularly around the themes of social justice, human rights, and climate change. As part of my broader project of engaging reflexively with the work of the museum studies, I have sought to hold this field accountable to its stated values and expectations. If there is a presumption that museums 'should' be politically engaged, the same must be said of writing about museums.

The issue here is that museum studies has no singular tradition of critique in the canonical modernist sense, which means we have no formal methodological framework to examine whether writing about museums is a form of intellectual activism. By extension, we lack the language required to identify and probe the impact it is making – be it on museums, on the field of writing, or on the broader sociopolitical context.[10] This situation has arisen partly because museum studies, like cultural studies, has 'committed itself neither to a set of particular methods or theories nor to particular objectives (is it managerial, populist, or critical?), although it does repeat a restricted set of problematizations, which, as we have seen, concern social ends as much as analytic frameworks' (During 2006: 278).[11] Rather than aiming to make a case for the establishment of clearly defined parameters, I propose that the absence of a discrete formal tradition is a double-edged sword that is both paradoxical and productive, and that the tensions implicit here are useful to keep in play for anyone interested in understanding or testing the limits of conventional forms of thinking. We can understand the paradox as productive because museum studies, like other cognate interdisciplinary fields (such as heritage studies, Sørensen and Carman 2009a: 2) that have typically 'borrowed' discursive tools to address their specific research questions, have done so in order to develop responses to critical contemporary issues without being constrained by particular traditional forms of disciplinary critique (a point upon which cultural studies has, for instance, insisted, During 2006: 278). The trick, however, is to develop these strategies and frameworks (borrowed or not) in a way that is methodologically rigorous, in line with stated interests in grounded forms of analysis and a commitment to social justice agendas. A further paradox of this dichotomy is, of course, that interdisciplinarity is not one thing and that it cannot be defined by opposition, where writing is, for example, understood as being consistent with disciplinary norms *or* not.[12]

Recognizing the construction and impact of 'fields' – assemblages of institutions, disciplines, collections, sites of action – has become an increasingly popular and fruitful process in anthropology, museum studies, and art theory and criticism, among other disciplines.[13] My use of the term here is general. I refer to interdisciplinary fields of research like museum studies or cultural studies that have evolved predominantly in the postwar period (although they may have links with nineteenth-century disciplines, these interdisciplinary forms developed, at least to an extent, through a process of resistance against postwar pedagogical approaches that were criticized as being out of touch and for replicating and strengthening problematic relationships of power, authority, and subjectivity). I also use the term 'field' to refer to the interface between disciplinary configurations and between certain spatial arrangements, illustrated, for example, by spaces created by the boundary between museums and their physical verge (see Message 2014: 4 for a description of the National Mall in Washington, D.C., as exemplifying this boundary space and Rabinow's use of the term as described in Chapter 3 and at Guyer 2016: 373). While verges have traditionally been used to separate people, practices, power, and ideologies, they are also spaces that are inherently impure, touching as they do both sides of the boundary and providing, in so doing, a space of interaction, transgression, hybridity.

In addition to my interest in disciplinarity and exploring the limits of such, my approach has been influenced by recent attempts to identify and theorize various 'fields', including work associated with the recently completed Collecting, Ordering, Governing: Anthropology, Museums and Liberal Government project. While the Collecting, Ordering, Governing project does not address the processes of contemporary activism that are my focus, it has been relevant for its analysis of the ways in which museums have historically acted on and been influenced by various interesting 'social worlds' and associated networks (Bennett 2015a, 2015b; Bennett, Dibley, and Harrison 2014; Bennett et al. 2017; Cameron and McCarthy 2015).[14] Similarly, although it employs a different set of theoretical parameters to examine governance than the cultural studies tools I offer in order to analyze resistance, this project has usefully built a case study of complex networks that existed across anthropology and museums at a particular historical juncture (the nineteenth century) in order to examine the limits, intersections, and processes of administration that occur through interaction across these zones. It shares my interest in examining the interfaces between those in power and those without (including activists known by contemporary social movement theory as 'challengers'[15]), particularly in relation to the role of culture, which is presented, pace Foucault, as a key interface, a transactional reality, that mediates 'the interface between the governed and the governing' (Bennett, Dibley, and Harrison 2014: 141).

Regardless of the specific theoretical angle adopted, the case study or site examined, or the historical era investigated, understanding museums as sets of relations or as 'assemblages' of fields and their constitutive elements (including the social networks between practices, materials, discourses, knowledges, and forms of administration)[16] is a useful exercise. Indeed, while I believe the terms and experiences of government and freedom should not be understood as diametrically opposed or dichotomous terms, it is critically important that any attempt to investigate resistance demonstrates a clear understanding of the application – direct and indirect – of power (particularly the formal apparatuses of 'social management'). This understanding can be facilitated by work coming out of the Collecting, Ordering, Governing project and its reading, in particular, of Foucault's account of liberal government 'as a set of knowledge practices and technologies that work through the forms of freedom they organize', the 'Latourian tradition of science studies and on the "archival turn" that has characterized recent revisionist approaches to the histories of anthropology and other collecting practices', and post-Deleuzian assemblage theory 'to analyze the agency of human and nonhuman actors in different sites of collection and in the passage of things, texts, and data from those sites of collection to centers of calculation' (Bennett et al. 2017: 4). It is also an approach that has its roots in contemporary reflections on anthropological theory and practice, which augments art historian Christopher Whitehead's Bourdieu-influenced contention that museums offer 'a unique site for a unique kind of theorizing, but such theorizing may well be inherently compromised by circumstance' (Bourdieu and Wacquant 1992; Whitehead

2009: 39). Complementing Bennett et al.'s exploration of nineteenth-century anthropology and museums in various colonial contexts, Whitehead's work addresses the engagement between museums and the disciplines of art history and archaeology across the same century (but in the context of Britain only). Although their respective approaches to rendering their fields of analysis differ from what is developed here, Bennett et al.'s focus on the ways in which museums act on social worlds (2017: 1) and Whitehead's argument that museums have played a direct role in the development of academic disciplines provide an important background context through which the disobedient museum – both as a book and a concept – operates.

The Disobedient Museum: Writing at the Edge offers a workspace that exists within a much larger complex of organizational units – 'fields' if you like. In bringing together various disciplinary approaches, it offers a space where resistant forms of thinking, seeing, feeling, and acting can be produced, along with a platform from which to theorize this process as a form of protest against disciplinary stagnation. It does not set out to achieve 'coherence of a set of otherwise disparate elements: objects of study, methods of analysis', an outcome associated with the traditional process of disciplining (Messer-Davidow, Shumway, and Sylvan 1993b: 3). Neither does it aim to turn conventional knowledge upside down or render it baseless. Rather, it aims to suggest that crisis of any scale can offer a generative function that contributes to a process of reflection as well as the ongoing process of re-forming ways of addressing knowledges, experiences, and the networks and structures – macro and micro – through which contact occurs. The disobedient museum sits counter to the understanding that museums 'move through social space interpreting, fusing, and fissioning as they are caught in the cross-cutting pressures of fields' (Fyfe 1996: 210 quoted in Whitehead 2009: 39). Rather than accept the idea that the theorizing that takes place within any actual physical or virtual museum may be 'inherently compromised by circumstance', my approach seeks to prize open and occupy the place of 'cross-cutting' (a site of disciplinary interface) with the aim of articulating what happens at this place. How do the multiple agencies that occupy this localized, compromised, and contested space react to the dominant pressures around them? What is the process by which this 'field' of engagement can be articulated for the purpose of elaborating the role that museums play (as a similarly localized/contested space) to impact on broader political contexts and concerns?

The approach presented here differs from normative modes of museum analysis that have tended to focus either on ways that museums have acted on the social world (an historical example would be the colonial processes of collecting, and a contemporary one would be museum-run community development initiatives) or the impact that external factors have had on museum operations (such as a change of government and reduction in funding or change in ideological position). More recent work on the relational museum (Gosden and Larson 2007: 5; Morphy 2015) has provided a way to bring these foci into a shared space of analysis by looking at the trajectories of movement and influence that can be traced across internal and external spheres. *The Disobedient Museum: Writing at the Edge* builds on this work but focuses on the spaces of slippage that typically 'fall out' of conversations about power, privilege, and influence but which are anything but politically neutral. It is methodologically important to recognize these spaces pragmatically (who is included or excluded by museum activities) as well as in conceptual and disciplinary terms because they exist as an interface as well as a network between text (object of study) and a context (field of action), as well as a range of other false dichotomies that are often applied to museums (inside/outside, public/private, theory/practice, and so on and so forth).

This book's interest in expanding methodological possibilities for articulating difficult conceptual and disciplinary relationships is unconventional for museum studies, which typically subjugates or makes the process of writing about museums invisible to the outcomes that museums aspire to or achieve.[17] Benefits of traditional museum studies approaches include highlighting the social and political impact of museum work and, in some cases, modeling collaborative research projects that involve museums and writers, often with additional community-based stakeholders and 'expert-citizens' (Third 2016; Sandell 2016). Despite these strengths, one motivation for writing this book has been frustration on my part about the methodological deficit that I increasingly see in manuscripts, journal articles, and theses affiliated with museum studies. Excellent research problems and questions abound and are often well identified by researchers; however, an overreliance on the same tired conceptual tools is commonly exhibited in written work. Rather than asking what other approaches might be most suited to addressing specific research problems (and what, concurrently, might the research findings reveal about the discipline itself), I am frequently presented with work that is silent about the methodological choices made or that adopts a generic interdisciplinary approach without providing a rationale for why the 'theory' suits the challenge or evidence at hand.

If we want to hold museums accountable for claims that they are politically or socially affective, we must also recognize and be accountable for the fact that writing evidence, writing methodology, and writing theory are themselves key elements in work that seeks to make a difference – be it in academic terms or for a social impact or political change. I am not asking to renew calls for tools that 'measure' the impact of our work. Quite the opposite, I am arguing that we need to develop more rigorous understandings and debates around what critique is, how it works, and what its impact and limitations might be in our field of research (Post 2009). This task requires attention to the basic, admittedly dry and difficult but fundamentally important, questions that include 'How does one write about the different modes of relating to the world as a researcher and what are their ramifications on what one produces as accounts of reality? . . . How does one integrate theory in the process of writing?' How can we make theory speak to social and cultural realities and vice versa? (Hage 2016). This approach also recognizes that forms of analysis that sit at the edge of disciplinary norms risk exposing the limits and shortcomings of such work – an outcome that is, of course, appropriate for any attempt to explore the legacies and potentials of disciplinary and inter-disciplinary work today.

The Disobedient Museum: Writing at the Edge has been designed with these questions and challenges in mind and as an attempt to draw attention to the importance and potential impact of critical writing within the academic field of museum studies. It also aims to highlight the relationship between our subjects (museums and political culture in this case) and the agency and positions we adopt in relation to processes of writing. Like the process of making museum collections, exhibitions, or buildings, writing is always about making and remaking representations, 'materializing the world and relationships within that world; because words do more than simply name the things for which they stand' (Webb 2016). Recognizing the ethical imperative of the writing we produce therefore requires recognition that writing is itself an inherently political activity regardless of whether we write to progress a political agenda or not. This book aims, as such, to set the agenda for a new approach to thinking about writing about museums and the engagement between museums and the contemporary social/political context within which they operate. It represents a provocation – as much to myself as a museum studies scholar as well as to others – to reflect upon and examine how we can more effectively address and contribute to the political project of culture in contemporary life. It articulates problems rather than solutions, and indeed I believe its contribution is initiating a process of self-reflection for our field. The process of answering some of the challenges and provocations posed here will not be for me or any individual to offer concrete solutions but will be likely an iterative and collaborative process that involves many participants. What will be important in future discussions is whether our work in writing about museums has made a difference in turning abstract principles into concrete concerns that both reflect and contribute to the movements that we seek to represent or engage with critically.[18]

In summary, this book provides a focus piece on the single concept of writing about museums. My intention is to resituate this practice so that it might have an influence on the field of political discourse by addressing culture as something that has remained largely unquestioned or unthought about in approaches more commonly taken to the genre. Rather than taking for granted the generally accepted definitions of the concept of politics (or museums, for that matter), my argumentative strategies have been designed to reconfigure writing about museums as a political activity that functions as a potential intervention into mainstream political cultures. My broad definition of politics comes from *Political Concepts: A Critical Lexicon*, which offers the 'view that "politics" refers to the multiplicity of forces, structures, problems, and orientations that shape our collective life. Politics enters the frame wherever our lives together are staked and wherever collective action could make a difference to the outcome' (Political Concepts 2011). As 'no discipline possesses any hegemony over this critical space', and as the contribution of culture to political change has been underestimated, my attention to writing about museums is a timely exercise.

The concept of disobedience is central to this political 'intervention' because of its ability to reveal the increasing difficulties associated with forms of insistent or embodied opposition, and because it can model tactical forms of subversion that articulate transgression within a political/ social context characterized increasingly by direct conflict over opposing political positions. Mobilizing Michel de Certeau's (1984) theorization of tactics and strategy, the disobedient museum offers a concept model as well as a description for a process of writing and critical engagement. Focused on processes that seek to transgress boundaries, it can be used to describe examples of political activism (Chapter 1), as well as processes involved in writing about actions and engagements (Chapters 2 and 3). Rather than offering a template or how-to guide or even a manifesto for politically engaged forms of writing about museums, the disobedient museum is, at its crux, a call for more methodologically engaged forms of writing and critical analysis about museums. While a case study of this approach will be presented in *Curatorial Activism* (Message forthcoming 2018b), which, as the companion piece for this book, examines a specific instance of political activism and museums in a current U.S. context, *The Disobedient Museum: Writing at the Edge* has been developed to set the key questions and theoretical parameters motivating the Museums in Focus series. I hope that this is a discussion to which many writers will contribute over the coming years.

Notes

1 Slogan from Occupy Finsbury Square as observed by Gledhill (2012: 342).
2 Social reform movements are defined most generically as a type of group action. Large, sometimes informal groupings of individuals or organizations, movements focus on specific political or social issues and aim to carry out, resist, or undo a social change. They can take different forms and can represent a variety of concerns and agendas under singular or shared banners. See Tilly and Tarrow

(2007: 187); Tilly (1978); Tilly (2008); and Bevington and Dixon (2007). For the relationship between social reform movements and museum activism, see Message (2014) and *Curatorial Activism* (Message, forthcoming 2018b).

3 *Knowledges: Historical and Critical Studies in Disciplinarity* (Messer-Davidow, Shumway, and Sylvan 1993a) is recognized as a key volume on the structuring of disciplines in academia.

4 Best and Kellner (1991) explain that 'where modern theories tend to see knowledge and truth to be neutral, objective, universal, or vehicles of progress and emancipation', postmodernism 'rejects unifying or totalizing modes of theory' as reductionist forms that 'obscure the differential and plural nature of the social field, while politically entailing the suppression of plurality, diversity, and individuality in favour of conformity and homogeneity'. Following Foucault, postmodern theories tend to 'detotalize history and society as unified wholes governed by a centre, essence, or telos', seeking to 'decentre the subject as a constituted rather than a constituting consciousness'.

5 My strategic use of disciplinarity, which focuses on highlighting the limits, flaws, and prejudices of the term rather than its integrity, contrasts with recent work by Dewdney, Dibosa and Walsh (2013), which proposes a terminology of 'post-critical' and 'post-disciplinary' (an orientation that is similarly employed by Fraser and Rothman 2017: 5). In contrast with this book's focus on writing about museums, Dewdney, Dibosa and Walsh (2013) target the role national museums have played historically in forming the art historical canon by isolating its aesthetic categories from the 'political' and 'theoretical' intellectual debates occurring beyond the museum (Dewdney, Dibosa and Walsh 2013: 106). Despite employing different terms and forms of analysis, we share some concerns, notably over the approach taken by museum studies from the 1980s (Dewdney, Dibosa and Walsh 2013: 44), the need for methodologically rigorous approaches (Dewdney, Dibosa and Walsh 2013: 16), and the need for integrated approaches to working with and across theory and practice (Dewdney, Dibosa and Walsh 2013: 221). The main methodological difference is their argument that 'in contrast to the disciplinary project, the post-critical seeks to formulate, confront and solve problems of the everyday through a dialogic method embedded in practice worlds. The basis of the position advanced resides in arguing that in the case of museology, the agency of disciplinary knowledge positions, based upon a critique of established, embedded and implicit knowledge practices of the museum, circulate in closed, self-serving networks' (Dewdney, Dibosa and Walsh 2013: 226). Rather than looking at the potential for disruption within existing models, they argue that it is necessary to move outside the modernist paradigms and narratives of progress, freedom, and rationality, suggesting that the 'new conditions of knowledge production and exchange have led many to believe that knowledge reproduced through single disciplines and even in their combination and overlap in multidisciplinary and interdisciplinary modes of research can no longer encompass multilayer realities and the complexities of their networks' (Dewdney, Dibosa and Walsh 2013: 245).

6 Mitchell (1995: 541) calls 'indiscipline' the 'turbulence or incoherence at the inner and outer boundaries of disciplines.' He says (1995: 543):

> If a discipline is a way of insuring the continuity of a set of collective practices (technical, social, professional, etc.), "indiscipline" is a moment of breakage or rupture, when the continuity is broken and the practice comes into question. To be sure, this moment of rupture can itself become

routinized, as the rapid transformation of deconstruction from an "event" into a "method of interpretation" demonstrates. When the tigers break into the temple and profane the altar too regularly, their appearance rapidly becomes part of the sacred ritual. Nevertheless, there is that moment before the routine or ritual is reasserted, the moment of chaos or wonder when a discipline, a way of doing things, compulsively performs a revelation of its own inadequacy. This is the moment of interdisciplinarity that has always interested me. I think of it as the "anarchist moment".

7 There are other approaches to understanding the relationship between modernity and postmodernity, including those that focus on the role of the 'contemporary'. See Chapter 3 for further discussion; however, it is, by way of introduction, useful to note the argument by art historian and theorist Terry Smith (2009: 5) that '*Contemporaneity is the most evident attribute of the current world picture*, encompassing its most distinctive qualities, from the interactions between humans and the geosphere, through the multeity of cultures and the ideoscape of global politics to the interiority of individual being. This picture can no longer be adequately characterized by terms such as "modernity" and "post-modernity", not least because it is shaped by friction between antinomies so intense that it resists universal generalization, resists even generalization about that resistance' (italics in original).

8 The methodology employed in this book builds specifically on Message (2014) and Message (2015) and has developed directly out of the concerns first explored in Message (2009a) (see Chapter 3).

9 This question has been identified by some museums, museum writers, workers, and advocates as urgent. Attempts to prosecute the case that museums can make for social and political change have proliferated since Trump's election, building on the groundswell of action generated by the Black Lives Matter movement and #museumsrespondtoferguson, a social media initiative that was started to articulate the role that 'museums can and should play' in response to the shooting of the unarmed African American teenager Michael Brown by a white police officer in Ferguson, Missouri, in August 2014. According to Jennings (2015: 97), 'the word "Ferguson" in museum discourse has come to refer not so much to the town and event as to larger concerns about race, racism, and the continuing lack of inclusion in our cultural spaces', also signaling a broader interest in activism by the museum sector that has also been debated in forums such as 'Should Museums Be Activists?' (MuseumNext 2017).

10 This is not to suggest that there is no precedent for *critical writing* (the distinctions between critique and criticism are explored in later sections of this book) but that museum studies does not determine a singular or unified formal approach, although it is the case that dominant trends or disciplinary associations exist in different university contexts and inflect the teaching of museum studies. Some programs and centers are aligned with anthropology programs, while others have emerged out of an association with sociology, art history, or literary studies. For example, Barrett (2011b) and Leicester University's School of Museum Studies 50th Anniversary International Conference (https://globalcontemporarymuseum.com) have offered accounts of the historical development of museum studies in the UK and Australian contexts, respectively. Although there are differences with museum studies (in the role played in the field's development by nonuniversity institutions and external professional associations, for example), During's (2006) observations about the development

of cultural studies programs and departments in university contexts offer a useful point of reference for anyone interested in further exploring the disciplinary (university) context in which museum studies is positioned.

11 I have here used a quote about cultural studies rather than museum studies to demonstrate that a characteristic shared by many interdisciplinary endeavors is a concern with social relevance and impact rather than discursive or methodological integrity.

12 Indeed Mitchell (1995: 541) argued that while 'the category of interdisciplinarity is safely institutionalized', this does not necessarily restrict the potential impact of research undertaken at disciplinary edges.

13 Sociologist Pierre Bourdieu defined the field as a network, or a configuration of relations between positions (Bourdieu and Wacquant 1992: 96), that can span and overlap institutions and traditions, meaning that any analysis of its effects need also extend beyond 'the field' or its products (material and intangible) to the interactions between fields and the processes that influence (and are, in turn, influenced by) those actions.

14 Like Collecting, Ordering, Governing, *The Disobedient Museum: Writing at the Edge* starts from the premise that culture is 'not expressive of an essential set of relations between a people, place and way life but is a conjunctural and pliable articulation of those relations that derives its distinctive qualities from the creative, form-giving capacity of the people concerned' (Bennett 2015b: 555). Similarly, both projects examine (albeit in relation to the different contexts of the historical anthropology museum and the contemporary museum-like space of reform movements and public protest) how government comes to act 'not "directly upon individuals but indirectly through their incorporation within culture" . . . in ways that allow a balanced apportionment of the relations between government and freedom' (John Dewey quoted in Bennett 2014: 151–2). Collecting, Ordering, Governing also builds on the work of anthropologists working on 'the relational museum' concept (Gosden and Larson 2007: 5; Morphy 2015), who similarly represent museums as points at which various epistemological and intellectual ideas and practices interact (and in so doing also act upon one another). In different ways, the approaches outlined respectively by Bennett (2015a) and Morphy (2015), for example, extend Clifford's (1997) representations (including the contact zone) of the place of the field within anthropological practice by enlarging the scope of analysis to include the interactions between the field and the multiple sites and embodiments of agency that come together in entities including those labeled 'anthropological assemblages' (Bennett 2015b: 153).

15 Tilly (1978, 2008) defines political 'challengers' as subjects who lack routine access to decision makers. It is important to recognize, however, that individuals can identify with or 'belong to' different groups at varying times. The demographic make-up of 'challengers', can, as such, be diverse and changeable.

16 Bennett (2015b: 142) offers the term 'anthropological assemblages' as a means of engaging with the:

> ways in which, in their early twentieth-century forms, anthropological museums operated at the intersections of different socio-material networks: those connecting them to the public spheres of the major metropolitan powers, those linking them to the institutions and practices of colonial administration, and those comprising the relations between museum, field and university.

17 A similar argument has been made of heritage studies, which has been criticized for its lack of methodological reflection. In their analysis of the situation for

that field of research, Marie Louise Stig Sørensen and John Carman (2009b: 23) explain:

> Having developed as an in-between subject and with its practitioners working in academic institutions, governments and 'in the field', Heritage Studies . . . has paid scant attention to methods. This does not mean that methods have not been used, but rather that methods borrowed from a range of disciplines have been imported and the forms and relevance assumed rather than critically assessed.

18 As per my title quote for the conclusion of this book: 'Movements are born in the moments when abstract principles become concrete concerns' (Cobb 2017).

1   Political protest

Figure 1.1 Person wearing 'I can see November from my House too!' sticker at Restoring Honor rally, National Mall, Washington, D.C., August 28, 2010

Photograph by Kylie Message.

This photo has been haunting me. I took it on August 28, 2010, at the Restoring Honor rally at the Lincoln Memorial, the same location that Martin Luther King, Jr. delivered his 'I Have a Dream' speech during the 1963 March on Washington, 47 years earlier to the day. Although it is one of hundreds of photographs I took that day, this is the image that stuck in my mind.[1]

The Restoring Honor rally was organized by Glenn Beck, a provocative and famously right-wing Fox News personality aligned with former

Republican presidential candidate Sarah Palin and the Tea Party movement. Although Beck had declared the event to be a 'nonpolitical' gathering
for American patriots wanting to demand that faith and honor be restored
to American government (Halloran 2010), he also claimed that its primary
aim was to 'reclaim the civil rights movement' (Beck 2010a; Beck 2010b;
Milbank 2010; Rich 2010). There was, however, little confusion about the
ideological leaning of the event among the many thousands of participants
and flag wavers at the Restoring Honor rally, many of whom brandished
Tea Party slogans and insignia.[2] Signs of ambiguity were similarly absent
among the smaller numbers attending the Reclaim the Dream march, organized by Al Sharpton and held later that day at the Martin Luther King, Jr.
Memorial construction site. Beck had reportedly scheduled his rally 'coin-
cidentally', without being aware of the significance of the day. Unable to
use the iconic Lincoln Memorial, the Sharpton-led march instead moved
from Dunbar High School (the first high school for black students in the
Washington, D.C. area) to the site of the almost completed Martin Luther
King, Jr. Memorial, close to the Jefferson Memorial. According to one
media report, 'Tens of thousands descended on Washington today for one
of the biggest culture clashes in decades – one that pitted an almost exclusively white crowd against one that was predominantly African-American.
Both claimed the legacy of Martin Luther King' (MacAskill 2010).

Beck's appropriation of the language of the Civil Rights movement to
serve the interests of a conservative and disaffected, predominantly white
middle-class cohort undoubtedly contributed to the right-wing populism of
the Tea Party rally. Criticized by some for 'hijacking' the legacy of Martin
Luther King, Jr., he argued a connection between the Civil Rights movement (that would be more logically linked to the progressive populism of
the Occupy movement that emerged the following year) and a white moral
panic more commonly associated with the 1773 Boston Tea Party protest
against taxation without representation. The latter genealogy is represented
widely in familiar Tea Party slogans, such as 'Silent Majority No More!',
'Don't Tread on Me', 'Taxed Enough Already', and 'Don't Spread the
Wealth; Spread My Work Ethic'. Beck's language also tapped into a backlash against political correctness, a perception that despite President Barack
Obama's inclusive rhetoric, the white middle-lower-class American mainstream was being overlooked. The Tea Party rhetoric can be understood
as reflecting an 'I want to matter too' mentality. Critical cultural theorist
Lauren Berlant contends that this rhetoric articulates a feeling of exclusion:

> I want my friends, my group, to matter. Who matters? Why should
> group x [for example, Black Lives Matter] matter more, or first, or
> get more attention? It's hard for the formerly optimistic and unmarked

whites to *feel right* about other people mattering before they do, because they didn't know that their freedom was bought on the backs of other people's exploitation and exile from protection by the law. They thought their freedom was their property, constitutionally.

(Berlant 2016)

Although a clear affront to many social justice and civil rights advocates and activists, Beck's approach to defending what he perceived to be the 'real' majority against the powerful elites and vocal interest groups that control the political system was taken from an artillery more commonly associated with left-wing causes (Lassiter 2011). It can be seen as a direct inversion of cultural studies theorist Stuart Hall's advice for the political left to make use of liberal institutions and ideas in order to redirect them to its own purposes (in Robbins 2016). By appropriating the language of economic equality as a universal right for 'all' Americans, Beck offered a kind of privilege or exceptionalism by association for those attendees at the rally who had, following a speech by President Richard Nixon in 1969, come to identify as the 'great silent majority' (Nixon 1969). Instead of inventing new political and cultural terms of opposition, Beck co-opted contemporary (and often liberal) norms that already existed. In so doing, he also denied or at least raised questions about the 'naturalness' of any genealogical links between the Civil Rights movement of the 1960s and Martin Luther King, Jr.'s speeches with the parallel Reclaim the Dream march organized by Al Sharpton.

   The politics on display that day were elaborate and antagonistic or defensive, and the imagery on the no-tax, no-big-government, no-health-care, 'no-bama' posters, banners, T-shirts, and other paraphernalia followed suit. The homogeneity of visual messaging evident in most of my photographs from the day is consistent with Walter Benjamin's observation that the real work of commentary and politics occurs not with evidence presented by the image itself but with the subsequent process of captioning, framing, and 'naming' its significance (Benjamin 1997). Berlant agrees with Benjamin's analysis, saying: 'It is as though the aim of a collective political event has to involve converging on a caption that converts [the photograph of] a historical moment into an iconic event preserved from history's contingencies, people's memories, and ambivalence' (Berlant and Greenwald 2012: 73). Beck was certainly aware of the impact of 'naming' the significance of the event, as was demonstrated in his subsequent media statements about the National Museum of American History's solicitation of materials from the rally for its the national collections, an exchange that he duly reported as an endorsement of his political position (Beck 2010c; Groer 2010; for a detailed discussion of Beck's claims about the museum's interest, see Message 2014, 2017). The symbolic 'universe' created by the elaborate staging of the event – that, importantly, was reproduced in most photographs published in media reports – created the impression that, unlike the participants wielding racist anti-Obama slogans, Beck's message was a middle-of-the-road one. The 'I can see November from my House too!' sticker is part of the symbolic universe created by the rally.[3] As the image shows, the sticker and person wearing it offer an impression of moderation that in a 'normal' context might appear extreme but that, in the landscape created by the Tea Party rally, came across as reasonable, thereby imbuing Beck with a credibility that would be less likely to alienate middle America. Obama also knew how to mobilize the center to achieve this effect (and sway swing voters), a point explained in 2010 by political commentator, Tom Hayden, who says that while the president had typically been criticized for being too right leaning for most progressives, he required 'the existence of a disappointed left as proof that he commands the center' (Hayden 2011: 267). Beck's image of reasonableness followed this strategy of appealing to the middle ground and was, as such, produced as much through its contrast with the extremist slogans ('America: Love it or go back to Kenya') represented by some staunch anti-Obama Tea Party members as it was by its opposition to Obama's 'liberal' views. In other words, while the 'I can see November from my House too!' sticker was sedate in comparison to the ostentatious visual gestures evident that day, it provided a like signifier for Beck's middle-of-the-road messaging that further normalized his rhetoric by producing the effect of a political continuum in which Beck was placed centrally.

In her writing on activism, American author Rebecca Solnit argues that full engagement by political activists (which includes the potential to mobilize others) requires the ability to work across ideological divisions, to occupy a slippery position of discursive as well as ideological liminality. Although Solnit (2006) was writing about progressive (left-wing) rather than conservative (right-wing) political activism, this is the approach used by Beck in his attempted recuperation of the language of Martin Luther King, Jr. Beyond the obvious currency to be gained by an association (however real) with the Civil Rights movement, his appropriation of the language 'of the left' was a powerful tactic for demonstrating the value of refusing, rejecting, or blurring ideological picket lines. It allowed Beck to occupy a liminal space where he could speak directly to people who identified with a variety of positions across the political spectrum. In appearing to take an approach that was inclusive of people of varying degrees of commitment, from moderate to extreme, the Tea Party at that moment succeeded in building a sense of movement – or alliance building. Obama's own approach to lobbying throughout his election campaigns was likely also an influence on this process. In appealing to people to act like 'the people', said Berlant

(2011: 238), Obama encouraged Americans to be politically engaged citizens involved in activities such as voting and demonstrating. He sought, said Berlant, to incite people to act 'as if their activism would bring about a change that was bigger than their new attachment to activism or to him' (Berlant 2011: 238). Obama's encouragement of active citizenship influenced conservatives such as Beck and further fueled the growing backlash by 'the left (people identified as anti-war, anti-class inequality, anti-racist, antihomophobic, antimisogynistic)' against Obama on the grounds that he was a 'neo-liberal market man without any left bona fides' (Berlant 2011: 238). While some elements of this backlash were manifested by the Occupy movement a short time later, the backlash was criticized by Solnit and others on the grounds that it alienated people who were not radical enough, including those who continued to support Obama, even if in a measured form (Solnit 2012).

Framing optimism

I attended the Restoring Honor and Reclaim the Dream events in 2010 to collect data for a book I was writing about museums and social activism (Message 2014). I had commenced working on the book sometime after Obama made his 'Audacity of Hope' speech to the 2004 Democratic Convention (Obama 2004) but prior to the presidential campaign of 2008,[4] and it was completed a couple of years after the Tea Party rally. The book's content covered a period from the late 1950s through to 2013, and investigated interactions between social justice movements and museums in the United States, focusing specifically on the Smithsonian Institution from the era of the National Museum of American History's establishment and burgeoning Civil Rights movement and including the early days of tribal Native American activism as it pertained to regional cultural center development. My initial aim for the book was to map a chronology of activism-based interactions between national museums and the public sphere across several decades. However, the process also led to an unintended outcome of profiling a period of optimism in public and political culture in the United States (vis-à-vis this lens of cultural politics/museum activism) that characterized the roughly seven-year writing period.

This seven-year period has been identified by many people – from Obama through to Beck (in his Restoring Honor speech, Beck 2010d) – as one of hope or optimism, partly, it might be suggested, due to a collective desire for it *to be so*. This desire to feel – or demand – inclusion and representation within and connection to political narratives reflected a contrast with the immediately preceding period, which Solnit characterized as one of tremendous despair and helplessness caused by the Bush administration in the United States and the outset of the war in Iraq (Solnit 2016a: 19). The social optimism of the period was spearheaded by Obama's campaign of hope. His presidency consolidated decades of activism and contributed to the political, financial, and legislative changes required to start the process of making reparations for past injustices. Reparations included a commitment to supporting the building of 'agenda-based' or 'identity-focused' museums including the National Museum of the American Indian, which opened with celebration and fanfare in 2004, and the National Museum of African American History and Culture, which finally came to fruition in late 2016, many decades after a complex lobbying and development process (Message 2014; Taylor 2011). New national museums do not come cheap, and they are always hard-won politically, so the bookending of this period by these and other similarly significant museum developments (including tribal cultural centers) indicates the existence of high levels of political confidence at that time.

It would be naïve to suggest that this period was universally optimistic. Political confidence produced out of change (of government, for example) can be a useful salve, a distraction from ongoing inequality. Causes for despair as well as for hope continued to coexist following the election of the first African American U.S. president, and it would be equally incorrect to assert that any political party or persuasion enjoyed any form of consensus homogeneity or bulletproof longevity. Support for Obama, even among his traditional base, had waned by 2010, with some conceding that his presidential performance was 'now about the politics of the less bad' (Berlant and Greenwald 2012: 80). Solnit shares this view, cautioning that although the 'bad old days' (of the Bush presidency, for instance) had passed, 'despair, defeatism, cynicism and the amnesia and assumptions from which they often arise have not dispersed' (Solnit 2016b). This statement also shows that despair is often an accompaniment if not a precondition for optimism. Instead of existing on a binary scale (for example, we are happy *or* sad, included *or* excluded), hope (or optimism) exists as – an often partial – measure of both. Solnit illustrates this point by arguing that optimism (or what she prefers to call 'hope') does not mean ignoring the moments of despair. It means 'remembering what else the twenty-first century has brought, including the movements, heroes and shifts in consciousness that address these things now'. This has, she says, 'been a truly remarkable decade for movement-building, social change and deep shifts in ideas, perspective and frameworks for large parts of the population (and, of course, backlashes against all those things)' (Solnit 2016b).

In contrast to Solnit's use of hope as a linguistic framework through which to engage with the complexities of the current era, Berlant's assessment is bleaker. She argues that our current political fascinations (with

Obama or Beck or Trump or whoever else) are symptomatic of what she calls 'cruel optimism'. A relation of cruel optimism exists when something you desire is actually an obstacle to your flourishing. We desire, for example, political change, so we attend rallies and marches, campaign on behalf of our preferred candidates, and vote at elections (we exercise our obligations and rights as engaged citizens, as Obama appealed for us to do). However, instead of delivering the outcome we actually want (change), our actions reinforce the structural order and preexisting political and economic conditions that preclude real change from being made.[5] Whether our preferred candidate or cause is successful or not makes no difference to these structural conditions. What is cruel, then, about contemporary life is our commitment to grinding away at it, hoping that as long as we do everything 'right', things will get better. In contrast to Solnit's insistence on the 'extraordinariness' and transformations of the current period (Solnit 2016a), Berlant (2011) sees it as being marked by bad faith attachments and the resulting 'ordinariness' of crisis. Instead of working to overcome crisis, the attachments that we have to 'good life' fantasies (our optimism, for example, that a good life can be realized by mainstream political participation) further fuel an impasse such that, rather than being extraordinary, crisis is a constant and ordinary feature of the historical present, as a period and a concept that moves across individual, collective, and political life.

Berlant's commitment to critique works to identify situations where individuals are not impassive, where they develop strategies for survival and modes of adjustment for getting by, even when the norms and conventions associated with obtaining a good life are no longer available or effective. Key to her argument (and relevant to my aims in the context of this book) is a focus on the ways that new forms, genres, sites, and strategies for navigating situations of overwhelming incoherence and precariousness can also create new sites of action. Rather than embodying direct opposition (which arguably implies acceptance of the authority of the term you might be ostensibly seeking to critique), the sites of action/acts of resistance that Berlant is interested in are often liminal and do not typically constitute singular instances of binary oppositions or antinomies (Berlant 2016, 2011). They are instead multiple, mobile, and transitory, and, importantly, they remain connected to dichotomized terms or positions, as demonstrated by Beck's subversion of the tactics of resistance usually associated with the political left on the one hand and by his pretensions to centrality and reasonableness on the other hand.

While the projects of Berlant and Solnit may appear contradictory at the outset, they come together in their aims and in some cases the structure they use to make their cases.[6] Both understand, for example, that achieving transformation requires a change in the means of production as well as in the ways we think and act in relation to the norms and conventions, as well as in their resulting outcomes or objects, and both use the example of narrative genre and storytelling to make this point.[7] Both are committed to methodological innovation and outcomes and recognize a point central also to the basic premise of the Museums in Focus book series, that 'A Good Account of a Problem Predicts Absolutely Nothing About the Value of a Solution' (Berlant 2016). Perhaps more than anything else, both Solnit and Berlant understand the importance of their work as being fundamentally about changing the conditions, the encounter, and the experience of meaning production with attention to the art of critical engagement and writing.

Why museums

Fast-forward another seven years from the Restoring Honor and Reclaim the Dream rallies to 2017, where we witness the inauguration of Donald J. Trump as the 45th president of the United States of America. The inauguration was an event of massive proportions that was accompanied by declarations on an even grander scale of social, political, economic, environmental, and cultural crisis. Despite the intention to mobilize people to exert their agency against the new president's initial actions – including his January 31 executive orders that put a temporary ban on immigration from seven Muslim-majority countries (Executive Office of the President 2017) – activism against his administration has also contributed to the escalation of a feeling of moral fear by Trump's critics and supporters alike (which identify different causes for concern). Although citizen-led forms of direct action aim to confront Trump's policies and behaviors, perceived as being the root cause of the crisis, an overreliance on the term 'crisis' risks reaffirming the political limitations (rather than the possibilities) of the concept. One such limitation is that it closes down possible spaces for dialogue and debate and establishes an oppositional standpoint that reaffirms truth/power dichotomies such as 'us' versus 'them'. This approach can have the perverse result of justifying and empowering actions taken by executive authorities such as police or militia (especially if one can call on emergency powers) (Bady 2013). Instead of creating the space for dialogue, the risk is that an oppositional approach 'suspends process and compromise, the possibility of alternatives recede, and the only truth becomes the terms of the crisis itself' – for example, the policing framework in which protest is represented as a disorder to be removed. Questions about 'what happens next?' cannot be accommodated by an all-or-nothing approach that also risks alienating supporters of the causes who are criticized for not being activist enough.

Although it is my aim in this book to argue for the benefits of social activism in the form of citizen action, including participation in marches and rallies, it is relevant to make the point that the polarized thinking that moral fear generates can be as paralyzing as it can be enervating. The risk is embodied by a press release for a seminar that was issued by the Carnegie Museum of Art in Pittsburgh soon after Trump's inauguration on January 20, 2017:

> In a time when fundamental democratic institutions are under assault, the question of cultural authority – its conditions of appearance and disappearance – is critical. As a trusted civic institution, a museum draws its legitimacy and interpretive authority from the academy and the disciplines it names and organizes. The legacy of the culture wars has eroded much of this intellectual authority. What remains of the politicized public space? What form can creative resistance take when institutions of authority disintegrate?
>
> (Carnegie Museum of Art 2017)

Captive to the language of opposition typical of moral fear (institutions are 'under assault'), this statement represents the authority of museums, other democratic institutions, and the politicized public sphere as having been weakened after years of embattlement and funding cuts. Although ostensibly interested in identifying new models for 'creative resistance', it sets up the requirement that progress is a condition of opposition after previously asserting that the institutions of governance that would typically be the subject of resistance have been weakened. In other words, it claims that resistance needs to target institutions that have no authority. This nonsensical statement was presumably written by a museum's press office with the purpose of attracting attention to the plight of the cultural sector following Trump's election. However, in adopting the language of moral fear, where the only truth can be articulated according to the terms of the specific present crisis, it emphasizes the urgent present situation ('text') at the expense of any broader information ('context'), which has been abstracted and thus removed from its terms of reference. In what might also be a symptom of the discipline's lack of self-reflection and lack of a tradition of critique (see Chapter 2), the statement reacts to the crisis but cannot acknowledge the role that museums have played previously in forms of cultural resistance and activism. This, of course, also further limits the possibilities for cultural activism that the statement is seeking to mobilize.

Despite or perhaps because of its shortcomings, the Carnegie Museum press release example helps demonstrate my argument that while the value of museums to discussions about activism is their ability to create discussions *between and across* fields of activism and governmentality (text and context), this value cannot easily be acknowledged or articulated according to current disciplinary models. An approach influenced by the borderwork of Berlant (2007) and other scholars working on subversion and liminal thinking is needed to more accurately explain what role museums – as places that increasingly aim to extend from government through community networks – have at times of 'crisis' and, by extension, what role they may play in campaigns of resistance. A new framework for exploring the value of museums to political change would also aim to contribute to changing ways of thinking and talking about radical innovation. Itself an act of subversion/recuperation, articulating cultural/political value according to terms relevant to community-defined standards of well-being works in direct contrast to previous government regimes of utility promoted under new innovation economies where governments demanded increasing evidence and analysis of the economic, social, and public value of research according to a framework that has not been developed against the knowledge systems developed by cultural work. Subverting the use of 'innovation' so that it refers to a differently articulated form of analysis is a form of intellectual activism that redefines and repurposes innovation to become a form of politically radical intervention that further impacts our experience and understanding of the broader world in which we live. Part of this task requires understanding of why museums are important to political organizations and activism alike and articulating this contribution in a way that escapes the binary utility/exceptionality of culture dichotomy.

Museums are uniquely suitable as sites to explore and develop new understandings about how social and cultural activism works for political purposes. Contra to representations of museums as fully politically complicit sites of authority, demands by communities and other stakeholders for greater outreach and equity in their work means that contemporary museums occupy an increasingly paradoxical space. Fundamentally caught between sites of action and sites of resistance (as illustrated by photographs from the 2017 Women's March on Washington, also Message 2014, which discusses support given to reform movements throughout the 1960s and 1970s by the Smithsonian Institution), museums are always already compromised. It is common for museums to be criticized from all sides on the grounds that they are not governmental enough (not maintaining regulations against protest or representing a political party line, again Message 2014) or not activist enough (for example, complaints that at its opening, the National Museum of the American Indian did not adequately represent all Native American communities). Occupying a liminal space, they remain connected to dichotomized terms or positions but do not typically constitute singular instances of binary oppositions or antinomies.

An alternative starting point for understanding the position of museums and the role they might play in negotiating crisis situations is provided by

Tom Boellstorff (2016: 380), who argues that 'rather than being anach-ronistic "mausoleums" set in the past (dusty and dead), museums exem-plify Paul Rabinow's concept of a contemporary site, where "older and newer elements are given form and work together" (Rabinow 2007: 3) . . . [A]ccepting this also allows us to "ask about the production of historicity in contextual fields of culture and power" '. Although this approach was not apparent in the press release by the Carnegie, it was evident in other state-ments made by cultural activists who appeared acutely aware of the influ-ence and intersectional work of museums across disciplines, geographical areas, historical periods, and experiences. About the actions planned for Trump's inauguration day, January 20, for example, a petition by arts work-ers, writers, and others released a manifesto that said: 'Art Strike is an occa-sion for public accountability, an opportunity to affirm and enact the values that our cultural institutions claim to embody'. J20 Art Strike activism was directed at museums (in the form of requests for institutional noncompli-ance with inauguration celebrations), but the expansive language used by press releases made clear the understanding that their call for a day of action would 'concern more than the art field' (Davis 2017; J20 Art Strike 2017a; J20 Art Strike 2017b).[8] The key point that this statement makes is about val-ues. While museums have historically contributed to particular understand-ings of economic value and cultural capital, in recent years the discussion, at least in history museums that promote social justice agendas, has shifted to include broader definitions of the term as something related more directly to human capital.

Addressing the museum as a set of influences, confluences, and agencies – that is, an assemblage of relationships and boundary zones – rather than as a singular monolithic authority is an inclusive response (allowing a hetero-geneous membership to be defined as taking part within the intersectional context as per the contemporary social context) to a contemporary politi-cal situation that is perceived as putting human rights at risk. Positioning the museum in this way (in relation to social/political forces) is primarily a political action, but it can also be understood as one that links ideas to more expansive descriptions of museums and cultural fields from the late 1960s. Performance artist and cultural critic, Andrea Fraser, has explained that, from this period:

> a conception of the 'institution of art' begins to emerge that includes not just the museum, nor even only the sites of production, distri-bution, and reception of art, but the entire field of art as a social universe.
>
> (Fraser 2005)

The definition/understanding of 'museum' that I use in this book is oriented toward political and disciplinary approaches to understanding, explaining, and holding museums accountable. I am less interested in the institutional specifics of any particular place than I am in its interrelationality, as well as the effects that are generated by museums and museum-like activities and the processes for intervention in social/cultural/political as well as disciplinary contexts (this builds on previous institutional ethnography/history in Message 2014). In producing, occupying, or contributing to dialogical in-between spaces (where they do; this is not a universal generalization), museums can have similar goals to the marches and protests that are often performed at their edges – specifically those goals of promoting active citizenship and engagement in democratic processes through community-led collaboration (Message 2014). Museums and reform movements also often draw from a shared symbolic artillery. The Women's March on Washington on January 21, 2017, for example, offered a museum-like spectacle of unity that was translated by media coverage of posters, slogans, imagery, and T-shirts into imagery showing the ideas of collaboration and community empowerment that are valued by many of the Mall-facing museums on the National Mall. I will expand on the analogy of museums and social movement activities in later sections of this book where I introduce the idea of 'dirty thinking' as a methodological approach for developing engaged modes of critique. Suffice it to say here, however, that the widespread adoption of the 'nasty woman' symbol offers an exemplary model of critiquing authority from within the terms used by that authority.[9] Rather than being 'outsider' activism, it enacts a refusal to give any ground – a refusal to move off a nationally symbolic place and with it a refusal to allow any easy rescinding of rights. It is disobedient rather than oppositional.

In the final instance, this book argues that what I call the disobedient museum happens in our streets and minds as well as in the institutions that typically celebrate and commemorate national lives. The disobedient museum project is first and foremost a commitment to action (intellectual, physical, or otherwise) and is thus not constrained by boundaries. It is a form of action that occurs throughout the whole sociopolitical context in which we live, extending beyond the museum walls into the streets, bodies, and actions of individuals and groups. The disobedient museum connects the political activism happening on the streets (context) with the representation of political life in our national museums and institutions (text). Intellectual and practical engagement discourse among museums, political activists, writers, and others – as symbolized by the Women's March on Washington and the affiliated J20 Art Strike but also including the

Restoring Honor rally – offer some models consistent with the disobedient museum project, but there are many more.

This is the time when museums go to work

This book explores different frameworks for writing about and understanding museum activism, intellectual activism, and cultural activism within a period explained as being continually in crisis. Unlike the earlier twenty-first-century period characterized by Solnit (2006) as 'dark', which needed to be combatted by the 'hope' that came to represent the subsequent era of Obama, the present day has been described as a kind of 'impasse'. It is 'not *another* day; it is an *other* day, altogether' (Ernest Gellner 1965: 67, reused in Guyer 2016: 374), where crisis, or a series of impasses, has become routinized. Rather than just being a condition of contemporary life, these have become part of the framework that contributes to structure our experience of life. An impasse does not necessarily infer a negative condition or a roadblock but arises instead from a situation in which crisis has become ordinary and constant. Berlant (2011) argues that the impasse functions as a kind of border zone that enables the creation of new sites of resistance at the same time as it demonstrates the limits of new forms of critical thinking. As we saw earlier in relation to Beck's activism, tactics of direct opposition are less effective in this liminal context than those of measured disobedience, defiance, or even a lack of action, or a refusal to move, be defined, or obey. This has also become writ large in the images of mass action following the election and inauguration of Trump, particularly in the women's marches. Aaron Bady's analysis of the occupation of the Berkeley campus of the University of California in 2011 by Occupy Cal (an affiliate of the Occupy movement) combines with these recent images to extend Berlant's point (2011) to make a similar argument:

> The modern sense of crisis, however, is rather different. To invoke 'crisis' is to declare an emergency situation, yet one in which nothing actually emerges: the threat is that something might change, to which the response must be a reiteration of the status quo. Instead of a moment of immanent critique – in which alternatives become manifest and change is unavoidable – 'crisis' makes criticism 'untimely,' as Wendy Brown puts it, unnecessary, unwanted, and impossible.
>
> (Bady 2013)

This impasse, where crisis is ordinary and unresolvable, cannot be a means to an end (it is not a moment of immanent critique). Rather, it is a condition of the cruel optimism that offers us the promise of change that only works to further strengthen the status quo. It indicates the urgency of finding alternative – but not necessarily outside – ways for resistance, particularly where institutional organizations and assemblages such as museums are concerned. To do this, I follow Bady (2013) in advocating a position of disobedience rather than direct opposition, where disobedience exists as an in-between/liminal term or site of resistance that provides an appropriate and relevant model for understanding the relationship between museums, government, and publics.[10] This 'disobedient' rather than oppositional approach is also consistent with Stuart Hall's recommendation for activism to focus on challenging the structures of oppression from a position of engagement rather than seeking to overturn them entirely.

The specific question here is whether, following Berlant (and Brexit, the 2016 election of Donald Trump as U.S. president, and so on and so forth), we now understand/accept the ordinariness of crisis as a way of life, and if so, what are our subsequent expectations of museums? How might/should museums enact accountability and responsibility in this shifted rubric? Certainly most museums have become accustomed to working within national contexts of crisis that are economic as well as ideological (Belfiore and Upchurch 2013; Message 2009b; Message 2013), but how might a discourse of disobedience rather than direct opposition provide a form of potential resistance for these sites that are themselves frequently represented as liminal contact zones (Clifford 1997) that enable engagement between diverse interest groups and conflicting agendas? These initial questions have led me, pace Bady (2013), to think about critique as disobedience – or, more accurately, as disobedience as a form of 'critique' – and what this concept might mean for politico-cultural institutions as well as our responses to them.

This theoretical context frames my approach to understanding how museums enact activism regarding social justice in order to analyze how museum studies scholarship extends or limits this goal. To do this, I examine a range of social reform movements and their strategies, including, for instance, the Tea Party phenomena discussed briefly in relation to the Restoring Honor rally in this chapter, and the Occupy movement (which is the substantive subject of my forthcoming book, *Curatorial Activism*), as well as a range of theoretical and scholarly approaches to intellectual activism (the main focus of this book). The disobedient museum is committed to agenda setting and the activism of writing about museums; it draws on a range of cultural, theoretical, and political authors and disciplines, from the literary (Berlant 2007, 2011) through to the more populist (Solnit 2006), including even the unlikely (Beck) to examine, on the one hand, the links that might exist between methods of critique today and moments of historical and disciplinary crisis and to ask, on the other hand, what contribution museums may have made to these modes of critique either as direct actors/players or through their activities of documentation and recollection.

Just as Jenny Pickerill and John Krinsky (2012: 280) have argued that it is important to analyze the Occupy movement to fully understand 'the political importance of social movements and the theoretical limits of social movement approaches', it is my aim throughout this book, and indeed a main motivation for developing the broader Museums in Focus series, to argue that we must understand the political potential as well as the disciplinary limitations and restrictions of museum studies approaches in dealing with social reform movements and actions if we are to properly hold museums accountable for their often stated goals of social justice. This is particularly important in the current Trump era, where, immediately upon election of the Republican, museum educator Mike Murawski adapted the work of writer Toni Morrison to claim, 'This is the time when museums go to work' (Murawski 2016a). Statements such as this have become commonplace and consistent with statements by the intellectual left like, 'We may be living through times of unprecedented change, but in uncertainty lies the power to influence the future. Now is not the time to despair, but to act' (Solnit 2016b). Whereas Murawski sees the urgency of action by museums as being the 'the urgency of empathy, social impact, and social action in museums today, focusing on 5 actions – that's right, I said actions . . . not ideas, concepts, or principles' (Murawski 2016b), I argue the necessity of critical thinking, engagement, and reflection on practice. This is crucial to ensure the continued relevance and contribution of museum studies and thinking to social agendas and concerns. I do not see this as being an either/ or proposition and believe our positions are complementary.

The central idea of this book is that intellectual debate and change is necessary to account for political change, and this can only benefit from an improved understanding of the processes that are continually unfolding, including understanding protest and reform movements as forms of process and possibility. Critique is a crucial element of this process because rather than denouncing the present from a more authentic position in the past or in the future, it 'reframes [the] problems we face today from another subject position, one that articulates norms and forms differently' (Deliss and Keck in Faubion 2016: 387). And yet critique – at least in the context of criticism about museums – seems to have typically withered rather than risen to the challenge at hand, relying on past models and languages of problem solving rather than looking to identify a new approach to and possibly vocabulary of critique. Where political institutions, activists, and museums have found themselves needing to navigate an environment that reflects 'neither the overdrive of the universal intellectual nor the authoritative precision of the specific. Rather, a space of problems. Of questions. Of being behind or ahead. Belated or anticipatory. Out of synch. Too fast or too slow. Reluctant. Audacious. "Annoying"' (Rabinow 2007: 39 in Deliss and Keck 2016: 390). Criticism in many fields (Terry Smith singles out the visual arts) has become 'conflicted and confused about the nature of its contemporaneity' (Smith 2016: 391).

This description suggests that the expectations we have of criticism are too great, too heroic, or even that critique itself has become a vehicle for cruel optimism. It suggests the continued preconception that critique should itself function as or generate crisis – not the kind of ambivalent crisis that Berlant and others says is typical of the present day, but a crisis that is resolvable and leads to productive transformation. Belief in critique as a positive crisis is consistent with governmental statements about the value of innovation, which should be radical and unrelenting. For example: 'Radical innovation can be considered as a system of critical and disruptive thinking about a specific condition or set of conditions in order to advance changes in practice' (Science Europe Scientific Committee for the Humanities 2015). The presumption here is that disruption is synonymous with large-scale regeneration. The premise of this book is quite different. I argue that developing the strategies and tactics of radical intervention needed to build an effective form of critique requires looking at the small-scale engagements with ambivalence and observing the actions of the current day. To do this, *The Disobedient Museum: Writing at the Edge* introduces the theoretical parameters and methodological challenges for the series by introducing the ideas and recent intellectual history of crisis and dissent as related to museums, heritage, and other forms of cultural activity, production, and phenomena and by probing connections between crisis and regeneration in disciplinary contexts. Drawing also on Berlant's insistence on problem solving, the book reflects upon the artillery of concepts and techniques that museum studies and cognate disciplines have offered for the practice of critique.

Notes

1   A note on illustrations: There was a strong temptation to heavily and richly illustrate this book in order to provide a comprehensive representation of 'museum-like' spaces of resistance and to demonstrate in visual form a genealogy of reform in the United States from the events of 2010 to the present-day women's marches and protests in the wake of Trump's election. However, I ultimately decided to include only a small number of key images taken during 2010 fieldwork at the Restoring Honor rally and Reclaiming Honor march in Washington, D.C., to retain the book's primary focus on writing, and to emphasize the significance of the personal, social and political relationships and networks that exists between

images (as per my discussion in the final chapter about Debord's concept of the spectacle (DeBord 1994 [1967]) and Charles Taylor's description of social imaginaries (Taylor 2004: 23).

2 On August 30, 2010, *The Washington Post* reported that Beck had told his Fox News viewers 'not to believe anyone else's estimates of the impossible-to-know headcount of Saturday's crowd'. Believe only his own number, which he confidently reported at 'a minimum of 500,000' people, 'the sixth largest gathering' on the Mall ever, Beck said, roughly the size of that other defining moment, 'Ronald Reagan's inauguration' (Stuever 2010).

3 Presidential elections are held every four years in the United States. Registered voters cast their ballots on Election Day, which since 1845 has been the first Tuesday after November 1. The phrase 'I can see November from my House too!' refers to awareness by voters of the forthcoming election, signaling an intention for action.

4 Obama set the tone for this optimism in his first campaign speech, in which he said (Obama 2007):

> In the face of war, you believe there can be peace. In the face of despair, you believe there can be hope. In the face of a politics that's shut you out, that's told you to settle, that's divided us for too long, you believe we can be one people, reaching for what's possible, building that more perfect union. That's the journey we're on today.

5 A similar argument has been used by Thrasher's review of the National Museum of African American History and Culture, which has, he says, tried to create the impression that it is a strong advocate for African American rights but which has in his view manifested a respectability politics instead of representing a benchmark toward real social change (Thrasher 2016).

6 Berlant conceded on one occasion: 'The *process* of managing the ambivalent feelings that come from active political commitment is fundamentally optimistic, and no one needs to be protected against that. Optimism is what keeps you in the scene as it veers between being joyful, stressful, and tedious' (Berlant 2008).

7 For Solnit (2016b), this means:

> Changing the story isn't enough in itself, but it has often been foundational to real changes. Making an injury visible and public is usually the first step in remedying it, and political change often follows culture, as what was long tolerated is seen to be intolerable, or what was overlooked becomes obvious. Which means that every conflict is in part a battle over the story we tell, or who tells and who is heard.

For Berlant (n.d.):

> This is a question of storytelling, remediating the stuff of paying attention, and of interfering with (without negating) the hierarchy of normative philosophical abstraction over other registers of knowing. I want to think about how, in these encounters, people endure what's overwhelming – being in the room with what's structurally unjust, affectively impossible – and how they find registers (genre, media) for floating the affective event that impacts their sense of attachment to the world and its terms of reciprocity.

8 During J20, some museums remained closed, some opened only to provide human services, while some opened but waived entry fees. For other reactions by museums and the art world to Trump's election, see Adams (2016); Davis (2016a, 2016b).

9 #nastywoman was a social media initiative that began as a protest against the then 2016 presidential candidate Donald Trump's reference to opponent Hillary Clinton as 'such a nasty woman' during the third presidential debate (Rappeport 2016).

10 Bady (2013) unpacks the term 'disobedience' to argue that it is 'an interesting concept, because it's different than opposition or defiance. It can be passive. It can be apathy. It's not necessarily even an action: the simple absence of obedience has a power all its own, disobedience as inaction or disinterest'.

2   Disciplinary crisis

Figure 2.1 Contested freedoms: Person wearing Restoring Honor T-shirt in front
of Lincoln Memorial during Restoring Honor rally, National Mall,
Washington, D.C., August 28, 2010

Photograph by Kylie Message.

Dirty thinking

This book picks up directly from *Museums and Social Activism* (Message
2014) and 'Contentious Politics and Museums as Contact Zones' (Message 2015), but whereas that work focused on what museums do and how

they react and contribute to political activism and social change, this book explores the theoretical context that frames the way writing about these activities occurs. The earlier work took a primarily museological/historical/ anthropological case study approach to identifying (Message 2014) and then articulating the interdisciplinary value (Message 2015) of the relationship between culture (museums), politics, and the social reform movements that have agitated and affected both. In contrast, the focus of this small book is on the intellectual context and recent disciplinary history of analyzing museum writing and museum practice. I also gesture at times to the aligned recent history of intellectual activism (although I cannot do justice to this rich activity and its history in the space provided). My main purpose in this work is to build on the case studies and conundrums raised by the earlier work to analyze the practice of thinking and writing about museum scholarship *as distinct from the practice of thinking and writing about museums.* It does not directly address instances of curatorial activism (which is the subject of Message 2014; Message 2015, as well as my two forthcoming volumes; for analysis of contemporary art curatorship and/as activism, see Bishop 2013; Smith 2015) or aim to give advice about how museums might become more activist institutions but attempts to articulate concepts and techniques appropriate for progressing social and political change through a practice of cultural and disciplinary critique relevant to museums in this second half of the twenty-first century. *The Disobedient Museum: Writing at the Edge* is, in short, an attempt to motivate disciplinary thinking/ museum studies anew, to reimagine writing (about museums) as an activity/ place where resistant forms of thinking, seeing, feeling, and acting can be produced, and to theorize this process as a form of protest against disciplinary stagnation.[1]

In recent decades, museum practitioners and museum studies researchers around the world have become keen commentators about transformations in public action and challenges to perceptions about inequity and injustice in the public sphere (Barrett 2011a). They have shown museums to exist as sites of public consciousness that are part of the dynamics of cultural change intersecting with both formal and informal spheres of political action, and they have led debates about whether museums have an ethical obligation to contribute to social justice issues, extend government policy priorities, or protest against human rights abuses (Sandell and Nightingale 2012). The commitment by individuals has encouraged museums to build strategies to become relevant to the community, part of the community, and attentive to representing the concerns of diverse communities. The period has also seen a closely connected escalation of claims made about the instrumentality of museums to source communities and stakeholder groups as well as governments (Newman and Selwood 2008; Peers and Brown 2003). Ideas of shared authority, empowerment through recognition, community collaboration, and political agency have transformed the field of museum studies and have become central to discourses espousing the social and economic value of culture.

These changes have arisen partly in response to actions that have occurred on site or against museums but have also been influenced by the remit of some national and community-based museums (some tribal cultural centers, for example) to build and represent the political reform movements that have both challenged and contributed to dominant national imaginaries.

At the same time, however, the argument that museum studies can or should make a social or political contribution relies on clear disclosure about the methodological tools and approaches employed by its researchers (the 'how' of approaching problem solving as well as the 'what' they talk about). Because museum studies has conventionally, like cultural studies, been unforthcoming when it comes to addressing issues of methodology (despite its privileging of process and its often innovative use of multi- or mixed-methodology approaches), it is necessary to present a compelling argument that centralizes and demonstrates the idea that museum studies is a boundary that is exemplary in its interdisciplinary approaches to defining its field of research. It has taken me several years to be able to articulate the view that museum studies is most effective when it observes and comments on museum interactions with the social context in which it sits (as per the case made by Thomas 2010 and others, see Message and Witcomb 2015) and that it is least effective when seeking to examine the intellectual context for its processes of writing and analysis. In other words, museum studies is good at analyzing what museums do and the processes by which they engage with broader social and political processes, but it is not good at putting the processes of analysis used to conduct this work under the same microscope. For some years I have thought this dilemma was due to the interdisciplinary nature of museum studies; however, I have more recently formed the opinion that it is caused – at least in part – by the (connected) lack of a disciplinary tradition of critique in our field. This absence has become increasingly evident as escalating calls for museums to become sites of social justice have required a correlating process of institutional self-reflection (which has, for example, been particularly evident in exhibitions about slavery in the United Kingdom and in the development of museums and exhibitions in the early 2000s that embodied remediation and reconciliation for past wrongdoing by museums against indigenous peoples by governments in Australia, New Zealand, Canada, and the United States (Message 2006)).

I make no presumption about where museum scholarship should take place or who should undertake it. Although 'museum scholarship' is a convenient term, 'writing about museums' is probably a more accurate description of what I am referring to (even better would be something that indicated a dialogical process of writing about and with communities, collections, museums).[2] It is a process of critical engagement that can be undertaken by anyone, anywhere – based in museums, universities, or anywhere else – and includes collaborative work. I am specifically interested in the conceptual and theoretical elements of this work (for the purposes of this book anyway), as I am aiming to argue that there is a particular approach to writing about museums that constitutes a form of intellectual activism. It is useful for the purposes of my explanation to distinguish this activism from social (community-based) activism or curatorial activism (internal to museums) in order to identify whether it can (or does) offer another pathway for or instrument of social/political critique. In other words, instead of conforming with more conventional approaches to *describing* curatorial social activism or change, the framework I am proposing here aims to provide additional ways of *contributing* to this activism. The kind of activism I am interested in investigating and developing a framework for will be of most interest to writers working at the edges and points of intersection and overlap between museum studies, cultural studies, public history, and social movement studies (sociology).[3] The latter has been criticized for its inability to develop theoretical frameworks and forms of analysis relevant to activists and the causes they represent (Message 2015).

While my project is a primarily theoretical and perhaps utopian (rather than abstract) one, it does lead to an obvious question about what the implications of this conceptual approach might be for disciplinary work, specifically for museum studies, which finds itself both defined by and in relation to stakeholders – none of which exist as singular or unitary cohorts or terms – that include museums, universities, governments, as well as 'the public' (constituted both by individuals as well as a collective notion) and community groups. It also raises the question of whether a cultural or political crisis is the same as a disciplinary crisis. While political or economic crisis often generate forms of social activism and protest movements and intellectual reflection, can a crisis occurring in a specific disciplinary context inform or contribute ways of understanding in another theoretical (or indeed social/political) field? This is a key question for this book. A broader aim is to provide museum studies readers with an overview of some of the ways the concept of crisis is used in a small number of cognate fields covering social, cultural, and academic spheres. This chapter includes a review of critical approaches in relevant fields (museum studies and contemporary art theory), which is followed by a section on social/political crisis and modes of critique. The purpose of this chapter is not to pit one approach against the other but to ask what happens if we bring these discourses about disciplinary and political critique together. Are the combined statements of urgency and concern – and their associated calls for action, disobedience, illegality, and boundary crossing – indicators that we have hit a postcritical turn, and if so, are they an indictment on scholarly activism of the past 20 years or more? These questions will be continued in the next chapter, which presents examples of what critique *looks like* in various situations, and offers an investigation of ways that crisis overlaps these fields and the ways that a response to crisis in one context (e.g., academic) might inform or contribute to the management of crisis in another (e.g., political).

Theory and practice

> The gap between theory and practice is only overcome in developing a practice in its own right [a practice that works at the intersections, at the point of crisis]. It is a practice to bring together theory and practice. It had to be done. And the vocation of intellectuals is not simply to turn up at the right demonstrations at the right moment, but also to alienate that advantage which they have had out of the system, to take the whole system of knowledge itself and, in Benjamin's sense, attempt to put it at the service of some other project. What the movement needed from us as part of their struggles of resistance and of transformation, then, was what we had in our heads.
>
> (Hall 1990: 18)

In recalling the emergence of cultural studies in the 1970s and the challenge of identifying the role of academics in social movements, Stuart Hall said: 'We never flattered ourselves that because we were studying postwar youth cultures we were nothing but street boys' (Hall 1990: 18). He was making a case for an engaged intellectual practice that would work at sites of crisis, at points where conflicting systems or ideologies intersected. This intellectual practice would bring together theory and practice with the goal of fully understanding the cultural complexities of the contemporary world and developing 'genuine social connections between cultural studies intellectuals and others who might arguably benefit from their intellectual capital' (Ang 2006: 185–6). It sought to critique the system – government, knowledge, economy, cultures – of which it was part. While Hall was clear that this intellectual work must have a civic function and obligation, this did not mean it would be 'populist', 'easy', or 'done without engaging with theoretical paradigms' (Hall 1990: 18). In refusing to give credence to oppositions between theory and practice (intellectual and activist) and inside and outside (systems of privilege), Hall's claim for cultural studies was the same argument being made concurrently by political philosopher Luhmann (1990: 141), that '[t]he secret of alternative movements is that they cannot offer any alternatives'.

I was reminded of Hall's comment about resisting the superficial appropriation of street boy style in the final days of 2016, a year that saw not only the continuation of global human rights abuses and environmental disasters, but that was made notable for many by the number of pop music stars who died. The media embraced a language of extremes, with websites such as *News.com* declaring 2016 to be 'the worst year yet' (Carlton 2016). Britain's vote to leave the European Union and the November 11 election of Donald J. Trump as U.S. president fueled the oppositional thinking, with a for-or-against rhetoric manifesting in calls for citizens to suspect their neighbors, colleagues, friends, even family members of duplicitously voting 'against' us/the presumed shared common good in the Brexit vote and election of Trump (evident, for example, in backlashes against women voting for Trump, Glanton 2016). *Artnet* declared 'Activist (As in: actor/ activist; musician/ activist; artist/ activist . . .)' top of their list of 'The 13 Most Overused Words in the Art World in 2016',[4] while American performance artist Amanda Palmer's statement 'Donald Trump is going to make punk rock great again' (Gonzalez 2016; Harmon 2016) articulated a view growing in the cultural sector that Trump's election would generate a 1960s style alternative culture (Murawski 2016a).

The mainstreaming of activism evident in the media's rhetoric around these events makes assumptions about what political action is and what it is not. On the one hand, it recasts political action as question of preference or taste and style (Hillary Clinton/Democrat or Donald Trump/Republican) rather than as informed critique of political governmental systems and, in so doing, provides another manifestation of the relations of cruel optimism addressed by Berlant (2011). On the other hand, the simplistic for-or-against approach to activism limits the opportunities for political engagement because it has no capacity for acknowledging that *no* action, inaction, disobedience, and transgression are also forms of critique. At once nostalgic for the 'good old days' of political protest from the 1960s, 1970s, and 1980s, this rhetoric appears to have forgotten the outcomes achieved by a range of other complex forms of political engagement, including sit-ins (which are fundamentally no-action activism). This rhetoric has also lost sight of the critical point that a mainstreaming of activism is *always* a good thing where it results in increased critical engagement by 'the people' with their systems of government.[5] Even the conservative tactics of Beck's Restoring Honor rally generated political engagement (also fueling Sharpton's Reclaim the Dream attempt later that day and interest in social movements more generally, including subsequent Occupy events). In contrast, however, Trump's shock election and the shock British vote to leave the European Union arguably occurred more as a result of a lack of political engagement. The media reported lower voter turnout than average for the U.S. election, and the EU referendum was dogged by a conservative campaign of nationalism and xenophobia riddled with images of moral fear about the continuing loss of the 'good old days' (a feeling that the 'good life' may have been getting increasingly distant rather than nearer). In other words, political change in these contexts may have occurred because people stayed home (United States) or did not fully engage with the political process sufficiently to understand the full consequences of their actions (Brexit) (Apostolova, Uberoi, and Johnston 2017; Center for Information and Research on Civic Learning and Engagement 2016; Kahlenberg and Janey 2016). In both cases, these outcomes resulted at least in part from feelings of extenuated alienation by individuals and groups (where identity is associated with collective ideals) from the political process.

The problem, then, with the mainstream media's post-Brexit/U.S. election prescription of a certain, singular version of activism is that it does precisely what Hall cautioned against. In taking a directly oppositional stance (you're either for or against the cause) and making a presumption about what activism 'looks like' (Hall's 'street boys'), it restricts the opportunities for a heterogeneous range of political engagement and risks further alienating those who are already lost to the system (nonvoters). It also, more problematically for the purposes of this book, limits the potential contribution for intellectual activism of the kind Hall and others have explored. Writing this book in the wake of these media accounts (and the events themselves) solidified my goal for its purpose – this book's activism, if you like – to challenge this discourse by making a case for the 'dirty thinking' that can happen when people enact critique of an oppressive system from within it. I do this by following Hall's lead and that of the cultural studies initiative of the 1970s which sought to 'address the problems of what Gramsci called "the national popular": how it was constituted; how it was being transformed; why it mattered in the play and negotiation of hegemonic practices. And our intention was always to do that in the most serious way we could' (Hall 1990: 17).

Thinking about writing about museums

The Disobedient Museum: Writing at the Edge sets the theoretical parameters and methodological challenges for the broader Museums in Focus series. I introduce the ideas and recent intellectual history of crisis and dissent as related to museum studies and other cognate fields (primarily cultural studies and the associated fields of contemporary art theory and criticism) by focusing on museums as sites that have traditionally been associated with governmentality and nation-building but that have more recently been ascribed as contemporary versions of a public sphere that enable inclusion, representation, and collaboration with previously ostracized or excluded peoples and communities (McCarthy 2011; Witcomb 2015a).[6] I argue against the popular presumption that museums are innately 'useful', 'safe', or even 'public' places[7] and contend that recalibrating our thinking about them might benefit from adopting a more radical form of logic and approach. Examining this problem requires engagement with ideas of crisis, dissent, protest, and radical thinking. It requires an intellectual openness and curiosity about transgressing disciplinary normalization on the grounds that this process has led to or has been associated with an absence of critique. It also means recognizing the flaws in the propositions by *Artnet* and Palmer, which imply that one is either an activist or not, contra the argument made by Berlant (2011) and Solnit (2006) and others that activism takes a wide variety of forms of engagement, across various spheres, including an intellectual one. Examining the problem requires investigating what an appropriate intellectual project might look like and understanding that there might be no answer at all or at least no easy answer to the challenges. Approaching the problem also requires engaging in a reflective, self-critical process to understand that any intellectual project is always implicated with processes of exclusion, inequality, and that it is always compromised and corrupted from the outset because of its affiliation with the 'inside' (knowledge/power, universities, government, economy, media, even 'moral majority'). Finally, engaging with this problem becomes a process of understanding the potential that this kind of corrupted, 'dirty thinking' has to show that activism can be effective when it works surreptitiously rather than antagonistically.

The disobedient museum is a dirty project because it sits on the interstice between theory and practice, is up to its (metaphorical) armpits in both worlds, and is a whore to both. Although it is focused on writing about museums it cannot be separated from the activisms that occur within the museum or world within which these act – indeed the intellectual activism that I am characterizing as dirty thinking embodies the point made by Hall about cultural studies (and that Fraser 2005 and Foster 2015 argue in the sections to come) that there is no 'outside', that we always occupy the potential for change, regardless of our primary position, affiliation, or locations. This describes disciplinary canons as much as cultural, political, or social institutions or apparatuses.[8] As Luhmann (1990) contends, alternative movements still define themselves in opposition to, and thereby legitimize, the system they seek to challenge. As such, *The Disobedient Museum: Writing at the*

Edge starts from the understanding that crisis and critique are cognate rather than opposing terms (the existence of critique does not imply the resolution of crisis) and recognizes, pace Foucault, that critique functions as a judgment of the validity of institutions and concepts themselves rather than just criticism of its products (such as public or cultural policies).[9] Following discussion in the first chapter about theoretical responses to contemporary political events, my focus in this chapter is disciplinary. Museum studies is a field that has grown fast. Some 30- or 40-odd years ago it emerged as a nascent interdisciplinary field without boundaries or clearly defined practices, but today it is recognized as making a sophisticated contribution to knowledge and national benefit across many areas of the humanities and social sciences. Following my argument that activism is not an action defined in opposition to any other term or action, I contend that value exists in unsettling mythologies around museums as safe places by arguing that the 'museums are safe places for unsafe ideas' trope (Gurian 2006: 99) has become a caricature removed from its initial intent. Further, I suggest that this 'safety' framework, while well-intentioned, has become a liability for museums on the grounds that it leads them to become sites of what public historian Edward Linenthal (1995) calls the 'comfortable horrible', that is, 'places that allow us to cringe, sigh, and rebuke, but not be challenged on how our own cultural beliefs and political systems may be bound up in the suffering of others' (in Lehrer 2015: 197). Focused thus on the hypothesis that museums are *unsafe* places – and that it is this which makes them ideal institutions/assemblages to investigate the complex cultural politics of the present day – this chapter explores approaches used by various cognate disciplines in order to force open spaces for the conjunctures and interventions that uncertainty and crisis can attract. My use here of 'unsafe' does not intend to overturn the dominant approach with another singular framework but seeks to counteract the credibility of binary thinking by showing that there is, in fact, no validity to the argument that museums can be either exclusively safe *or* unsafe. As well as being influenced by the broader social/cultural feeling of increasing unease addressed in the preliminary chapter of this book and my increasing concern with polarized media discourse about the nature of activism, the shift of attention has also come about as a response to museum activism within and against museums.

In the final instance, this chapter aims to map the relationship between academic theory and cultures of activism in museums and sociopolitical contexts in order to establish pathways for investigating connections among crisis, critique, and regeneration in disciplinary contexts. It investigates the requirements and limits of museum studies and relevant disciplines in the practice of critique and attempts to articulate some interdisciplinary concepts and approaches appropriate for analyzing and perhaps progressing social and political change through cultural and disciplinary critique in the second half of the twenty-first century. To do this I start by examining whether (and how) museums have contributed to the activity of agenda setting for debates over cultural crisis. This is an important step in the process of understanding why debates about disciplinary dissent have typically been absent from museum discourse. This question aims to put the discipline itself under the microscope in order to encourage a process of redefining critical museum writing. While there are any number of expectations we make about our subject of study (that is, museums, particularly when we hold them accountable to ideas of being safe places and the like), what are the expectations, if any, associated with the practice of critical writing about museums? Although there is no tradition in museum studies for writing about disciplinary crisis, can the academic discipline of museum studies provide – or be expected to provide – a form of critical writing that can itself impel change (where change might occur in a social context or else in a museum or within the discipline's practices of writing)?[10] Understanding whether this is an appropriate or possible goal requires a shift in thinking. Instead of responding to (objectifying) a crisis as an external event, it might mean recognizing that – in terms of the models it provides for the practice of critical writing – the field of research is itself in a period of crisis worthy of critique.

A groundswell of interest in the concept of crisis is becoming evident in the context of museum practice. Most often the emphasis focuses on the way museums respond to crisis, although there is an increasingly accompaniment of calls – by activists within museums and external to them – for museums to act in provocative or agentic ways, for museums to 'be' the crisis. These calls have built on previous representations of museums as 'safe places for unsafe ideas' and from escalating claims that museums embody a kind of politically informed practice. The risk is that such demands for activism reflect the superficial media rhetoric that 'we're all activists now' (Miah 2009), as suggested by statements discussed at the outset of this chapter and as perhaps exemplified by *Time* magazine's 'person of the year' for 2011 being awarded to 'the protester' (Power 2011). However, this interest in activism usually does not extend to asking what 'political' activism or being activist might mean in this context. If we extend this line of questioning (as Ang 2006: 184 has done for cultural studies) to museum studies – as providing a form of critique to address this practice – we can ask what ways can museum studies, as a predominantly academic practice, have a political impact or civic impact?

This book can provide no more than a passing mention of some examples of museum work that I see as making a relevant contribution to this discussion,[11] as my real interest is in examining how a process of critical engagement can be reflected in the ways we think and talk and write about this practice. I speak from the position of an insider. After more than 20 years of working in this field, I have more questions than answers. One thing I have come to believe, though, is that our key words of 'critical' and 'engagement' demand participation rather than observation; they demand recognition that, as writers, we are also part of the crisis (which is an opportunity as much as a challenge, possibly more). What has not been considered in the context of our field – as a result, I believe, of insufficient questioning or analysis of mythologies about museums as 'useful' places (that is, places of governmentality and instrumental reason, even extending to include socially progressive agendas such as multiculturalism, as argued by Bennett 2005) – are questions about what the implications of crisis are for our discourse as well as for the museums we study. How do we address what is happening, particularly in disciplinary terms, when the discipline has no framework or language for assessing its own engagement with or indeed state of crisis. What is the relationship between crisis, as an action or event, and critique, as a process of analysis? Is there an implied causality at work here (does critique occur only after the resolution of a crisis), and what framework does our discipline use to explain these terms and relationship?

These are complex questions that have no precedent in museum studies, despite the field's increasing interest in offering museums as sites of interface or interaction (even interference) with cultural and political controversy and crisis, and its subsequent, related aims of mobilizing crisis in narrative constructions to mark out a 'moment of truth' as a means to think 'history' (Roitman 2012) where museums are both a condition of and witness to current and past events.[12] This book aims to initiate dialogue about what a language and approach for talking about crisis – broadly in museums and society, but specifically within the discipline – might look like. This conversation requires considering how crisis and the language of crisis can be constituted as an object of knowledge (Roitman 2012) to examine how language can work to form 'strategies' in some cases and 'predicaments' in others (Foster 2015: 2). The approach I take to starting this conversation requires recognition that terminology can orient practices without regulating them (Foster 2015: 1) and the reminder that writing is never politically benign.

Committed to the idea that writing is not just a process of description, objectification (attributing or revealing meaning), or affirmation but is a 'collective project' that speaks often too implicitly about its own perspective, power, and privilege, I contend that the process of writing is part of what I consider to be the disobedient museum project, as well as a central tool in the process of dirty thinking. 'Disobedience' becomes a central term/ strategy in this project because of its affiliation with transgression and crisis rather than with opposition and resolution. By refusing to respect boundaries and playing on the edges of acceptability, disobedience refers to actions that cannot be absorbed easily into civil discourse and cannot be either incarcerated or recuperated by social norms or legal systems. Disobedience is like counting cards. It is not illegal but is playing dirty to beat the system. Disobedience always evades being made socially legible (Bady 2013) and can be linked to what Judith Butler (1993: 138) argues is a 'crisis over what constitutes the limits of intelligibility'.

The disobedient museum project is a provisional and process-oriented attempt to come to terms with some of the processes and goals embodied within activism in, at, and against museums and other cultural sites – including writing itself, as a site of action. It is a process of intellectual activism that in some respects follows from Hal Foster's approach for engaging critically with contemporary art and contemporary art criticism, about which he says his goal is: 'not to apply theory, much less to impose it, but to extract some concepts embedded in some practices, and when appropriate to point to parallels in other disciplines along the way' (Foster 2015: 3). This point is reiterated by Aaron Bady (2013), who has similarly argued that critique must always be understood as a practice directed at some instituted practice, discourse, episteme, institution and that 'loses its character the moment in which it is abstracted from its operation and made to stand entirely alone as a purely generalizable' expression. Foster and Bady both make a case for an intellectual activism that is locally grounded (politically engaged/involved) but that is also valuable for the contribution it makes through its critique of the system or situation being protested. Although writing nearly 20 years after Hall's statement quoted at the outset of this chapter, Foster and Bady both reiterate the cultural studies academic's argument that intellectual activism is a practice in its own right that brings together theory and practice, that offers an attempt to put 'the whole system of knowledge' at the service of social/political/institutional critique (Hall 1990: 18). What I am arguing is for us to take this approach one step further, to use it for the purposes of disciplinary (self-) critique.

This book proceeds from here in the following way. I make my case in conceptual theoretical terms in this chapter before moving in the next chapter to offer one approach toward a practice of resistant writing/dirty thinking for possible future use by scholar activists seeking to write about crisis in museums, crisis in the world, or crisis in the discipline. The present chapter has three sections. Starting with an appraisal of the current state of the field of museum studies, it then moves to take a closer look at crisis – political, social, and disciplinary – before concluding by considering the utility of disobedience for the project of writing about museums and social justice.

Bad new days?[13]

Conceptually, this book recognizes the growing trend of authors to address museums as 'ideas', and aims to provoke them to critically explore what this trope actually means. Positioning (or 'knowing') museums as essentially

ideas or collections of ideas does not help bring them into focus or help articulate political associations, implications, or bias. Indeed, the rhetoric around
these approaches has distracted attempts to disaggregate the complex parts
of the assemblage that constitute museums. The challenge is highlighted by
a recently published volume, *From Museum Critique to the Critical Museum*
(Murawska-Muthesius and Piotrowski 2015), which argues that changes
have occurred in museum practice as a result of museum studies but does
not question what implications the changes in museum practice might have
on the process of analysis that is used by museum studies. Despite including a range of valuable case studies, the volume is framed by an analytic
approach that stops short of asking the vital questions: How has museum
studies responded to a changed critical museology and political landscape?
How has our approach to writing critique changed in the face of our changed
subject?

The lack of critical self-reflection evident in much recent museum scholarship is an oversight by scholars whose work demands self-reflection
and political engagement from the museums they critique. There needs
to be greater attempts to understand the relationality between writing and
museum work so that we can better explain the feedback between museums and writing and between writing and museums. Museum critique does
not just occur before or after museum practice but is itself potentially an
important partner/participant in the process of critical museology. The risk
of attributing causality (as evident in the title *From Museum Critique to the
Critical Museum*) rather than recognizing an ongoing reciprocity is that it
reaffirms distinctions between theory and practice. Speaking about forms
of institutional critique in the context of the art museum, conceptual artist
Hans Haacke (1983: 152) argued that 'artists [and/as activists] participate
jointly in the maintenance and/or development of the ideological make-up
of their society. They work within that frame, set the frame, and are being
framed'. Demonstrating an awareness of this relationship – that we are
coproducers of meaning regardless of who does what when – is particularly
important as collaboration between writers, curators, artists, and institutions
becomes an increasingly valuable and normalized form of critical practice
(Sandell 2016). *The Disobedient Museum: Writing at the Edge* is concerned
with methodology and interpretation and is, to borrow Rita Felski's agenda
(for literary criticism), 'not conceived as a polemic against critique' (Felski
2016: 5). Rather it seeks to 'submit critique to examination in a way that
might either allow us to strengthen its methods and rhetoric, or to find new
modes of politically progressive intellectual work that might be blind spots
of critique's style of thinking' (Selisker 2016). It encourages a broader lens
be taken to our engagement with museums as a way of identifying socially
and politically embedded forms that emphasize description, persuasion, and
action.

It is not, in other words, enough to simply agree that 'museums *are* good to think', a truism that has been misappropriated extensively since it was proposed by Arjun Appadurai and Carol Breckenridge in 1992 and that has provided a convenient framework for scholars to employ without examining whether it is the most suitable one for their research questions. Instead we need to ask how, why, and what these 'ideas' are before we can assess how 'good' or 'safe' or 'useful' museums are or might be. In doing this, we need to ask questions about the purpose of our discipline itself: Is it change-oriented? If so, what kind of change is it seeking to effect? In what context? How can change be initiated – what are the methods and language for this project? Who are we talking to or trying to persuade, and what approaches are suitable for building bridges of communication (Selisker 2016)? Critical analytic thinking associated with the cultural/political turn of humanities disciplines (literature, history, and anthropology among them) through the 1980s and 1990s has developed in subsequent decades to address or argue over many of these questions (Felski 2016).

While many of the key political concerns of activists or writers arguing for a postcritical stance have not been overcome in a museum studies context, there exist in other fields examples of recent work that is 'self-consciously examining the institutional situations of literature, literary and cultural studies' (Selisker 2016).' Such work includes new sociologies of literature, criticism, and what Scott Selisker (2016, discussing Felski 2016) has called 'the compelling mixtures of critique and advocacy we find in the new university studies . . . much of this refreshingly self-reflexive work imports most of what's best about critique and pushes it in new directions, and in narrative frames that emphasize description, persuasion, and action'. Although there is no space in this short book to explore this history of traditions and their renewal, it might benefit museum studies scholars to consider the intellectual history of critique as a form of public history. This would include revisiting the work of Stuart Hall and other 'resistant' writers who – including Appadurai and Breckenridge – worked to critically reassess disciplinary canons and their mechanisms, as well as the core questions that motivated their work, work that was described at the time in the following terms:

> Alternative routes to knowing, understanding, critiquing and confronting the cultural terrain of late capitalism and the cultural logic of the late twentieth century world are being mapped in the midst of intense theoretical and political negotiations, debates and contestations over how to construct a more decolonized study of humankind, a more authentic study of humanity's common ground as well as its historical contingency and embedded differences.
>
> (Harrison 1993: 401)

We may today be in an '*other* day, altogether' from the one just described, but, as the debates around the Brexit vote and Trump's election demonstrate, our modes of critical analysis and engagement have yet to reflect the changed order of contemporary life and the ordinary role of culture within this. For Foster (2015), this constitutes a 'postcritical' day.

A review of museum studies literature over the past 30 years or so similarly reflects how the intellectual shifts and 'turns' representative in cultural and critical studies fields – structuralist (museums as text), ethnographic (community initiated, participant observation), Foucauldian, 'post-Deleuzian' (Bennett et al. 2017: 4), and so on and so forth – have influenced how we write about our subject. However, despite our ability to adopt and explore these approaches for the purposes of analyzing our subject – museums – we have not typically taken a mirror to our own practice, which has meant that we are now ill equipped for addressing an 'other day' of continual crisis that our museums – and ourselves – are now challenged on a continual basis to work with and respond to. Some will see the disobedient museum project as an esoteric one; however, I contend that writing is a political project and that holding our practice of writing accountable to the same terms that we increasingly expect of museums is an urgent endeavor. It is influenced by the idea and potential impact of practices of institutional critique explored by Haacke and other artists in the 1960s and 1970s and extends Andrea Fraser's argument (2005), which provides a more nuanced and compelling explanation of the current-day crisis as a continuation of previous decades of activism associated with practices of institutional critique. Fraser's argument corresponds with the view of crisis as a continuum rather than as the break that Foster suggests, suggesting 'every time we speak of the "institution" as other than "us", we disavow our role in the creation and perpetuation of its conditions. It's not a question of being against the institution: We are the institution' (Fraser 2005).

Fraser says that although there may be no clear inside/outside distinctions today (no alternative to mega museums and global markets), this does not mean that there is no possibility for artists or activists to critique the political, conceptual and organizational structures and affiliations of museums. Indeed, the call she makes in her essay is for a re-assessment of the history and aims of institutional critique, as well as an examination of the role it may play in the present. The backlash against criticism that Fraser reacted to is partly due to a falling out of favor of structural approaches to critique in the face of more grounded forms of analysis (Felski 2016). The drop in popularity resulted, in part at least, from the typical association of criticism with an authority gained from a dispassionate tone 'that provides the critic with enough distance to identify and interrogate what seems like common sense' (Mullins 2015).[14]

The Disobedient Museum: Writing at the Edge seeks to explore whether a critique focused on and identified with museum studies has the potential to redefine a form of grounded critique that rejects the (modernist) 'distance' of scholarship in favor of an intellectual activism that positions the writing about museums as a heterogeneous practice of engagement with political structures. This approach is ideally suited to a study of museums as inherently entwined with the processes and governance of social and political life across all fields of cultural, community, and individual politics. Museum studies is, thus, ideally placed to develop a form of critique consistent with Bady's argument about the interdependence of critique and governance, both of which are, in his view, 'unthinkable without the other' (Bady 2013; see also Bennett et al. 2017). This approach would redefine the work of the writer away from being focused on replicating existing models or commentary to exploring forms of analysis/interpretation that take place against individually defined and articulated sets of goals. Of course, the lack of objectivity implied by this practice will not be for everyone, but, as museum scholars have argued at least since the culture wars period of the 1990s–2000s, museums have likewise never been politically neutral sites, and it is increasingly the work of museums (and, I am thus arguing, the work of writing about museums) to not just demonstrate the political implications (power and privilege) of their work, institution, and networks but to actively counteract this by making political statements appropriate to their work. This approach allows us to understand critique as being itself a social activity as well as a socially embedded process (Felski 2016; Mullins 2015; Selisker 2016).

The trend to address museums through a framework of controversy has been transformed since its surge of popularity in the late 1990s history/culture wars period to now focus on museums and human rights, specifically as a result of writers who have investigated ways that museums have represented or responded to increasing social interest in equality, human rights issues, and concepts of social justice (for example, Lehrer 2015; Lonetree and Cobb 2008; Onciul 2015; Sandell 2016). These works have employed interdisciplinary methods and have been influenced by the growing groundswell occurring in museum practice toward acting out of social justice concerns. 'Radical museology' (Bishop 2013) and 'punk museology' (Whitehead 2016), as well as curatorial activism, are becoming familiar terms used to guide and explain the practice of this kind of museum work. A new volume edited by museum studies scholars Richard Sandell and Robert Janes (forthcoming 2018) indicates the growing popularity of 'curatorial activism' (also see Message 2014) and exemplifies the contribution that practice-based activism within and at museums can make culturally and socially. Sandell and Janes explain the goal of curatorial activism as being able to 'elucidate the largely untapped potential for museums as key intellectual and civic resources to address inequalities, injustice and environmental challenges'. They highlight important work that has been developed in response to the groundswell of activism being provoked by the museum sector as well as the broader communities within which it operates. *The Disobedient Museum: Writing at the Edge* complements their focus on museums as sites of activism by arguing that museum studies should likewise be considered a site of action. Whereas they examine 'the relationship between museums and activism – campaigning, action, and advocacy by both practitioners and external organizations with activist goals and ambitions that both engage and impact museums' – my focus is on the theorization of this relationship and activities by the discipline of museum studies, with the aim of expanding the potential impact that intellectual activism coming out of this discipline might have on our social and political, as well as cultural lives.

The key point that emerges from any review of literature in the field is that museums and museum studies are and have always been political. I am not, in this short book, going to offer a detailed overview, synopsis, or audit of museum studies but instead seek to theorize the work of 'museum studies' to understand the kinds of work museum studies (writing about museums) is or is not doing in the construction of critique – that is, how it constructs narrative forms that account for interactions between museums and social, political (and even disciplinary) crisis. Likewise, my aim is not to demonstrate that museum studies signifies something 'new' in contemporary narrative accounts (this would be to buy into 'innovation' discourses associated with governmentality) or that it now has a novel place in the history of ideas. What I will explore is how writing about museums is constituted as an object of knowledge and the contributions its discourse can make to public, professional, and political understandings about museums. My argument is based on museum studies literature published specifically in the last 20 years for the reason that this period coincided with a spike in popularity for the discipline that resulted from a range of factors, including the implication of museums in the so-called history and culture wars in countries including Australia, the United States, the United Kingdom, New Zealand, and Canada.

The exchange between museums, topical affairs and controversies throughout the 1990s and 2000s (and beyond) coincided with an increase in the use of critical theory to discuss ideas relevant to diverse public spheres by Western theorists on the one hand and, on the other, an increasing awareness by governments and policy makers of the potential usefulness of museums for political advantage. The interaction between museums and government agendas has been widely addressed by scholars, who generally agree in their assessment that these parallel streams, despite being fundamentally at odds with each other in terms of where they attribute agency and authority (usually with 'the people' *or* with 'the government' but rarely both), culminated in heightening general understandings about the political nature of museums. An extensive body of work from this period examines this phenomenon (Bennett 1995; Clifford 1997; Luke 2002; Macdonald 2006).

Current trends in museum studies – as represented by Murawska-Muthesius and Piotrowski (2015) and Sandell and Janes (forthcoming 2018) – build on this scholarship and continue to be influenced by concerns about social justice and community building, as well as by public policy-oriented approaches (also see Belfiore and Upchurch 2013; Gray 2011). This recent period might be understood as representing attempts to bring the discourse of utility (governmentality) and the rhetoric of exceptionalism ('arts for art's sake') into closer conversation and in so doing presents a challenge to previous ways of understanding museums, as well as their relationships with society and forms of governance and resistance. However, despite its concern with cultural processes on the one hand and politics on the other, writing about museums often continues to struggle with how to identify and then to conduct research at the actual interface between politics and museums (Clifford 1997 is a notable exception, but see critique by Boast 2011: 62, 67). This struggle might be understood in some respects as itself being a productive outcome reflective of cultural processes. However, it has also created a disciplinary gap that has contributed to the argument that culture and the arts form an example of minor politics that is of low priority in the realm of political decision making (Gray 2002: 78).

Even while the culture wars drew attention to heightened popularity and support for museums and cultural endeavors, the extreme (either/or) thinking that characterized much mainstream media representation (art *or* politics) in the 1990s–2000s contributed to produce a crisis of sorts for museum studies. It is possible, for example, that even where scholars were critical of a museum they may have been disinclined to articulate this response publicly for fear that it might generate more grist to the mill of conservative calls for funding cuts and threats of government censorship. A protective approach to writing about museums may have itself been a reaction to a battered curatorial practice that, in the period following the culture wars, is believed to have suffered a kind of professional anxiety in some instances, which manifested in politically conservative exhibition making (Luke 2002; Message 2009b). Because of its longer tradition of disciplinary reflection and professional criticism, conflict between art and politics is more evident in the cognate field of contemporary art theory than museum studies. Foster's assessment of the impact of the culture wars period is that critical scholarship in the field of contemporary art criticism following this period has languished. 'Bullied by conservative commentators', he says, 'many academics no longer stress the importance of critical thinking for an engaged citizenry, and, dependent on corporate sponsors, many curators no longer promote the critical debate once deemed essential to the public reception of difficult art' (Foster 2015: 115). He is of the view that the practices associated with institutional critique have been recuperated into the mainstream art-historical economic systems and structures that they once rallied against. Foster's point is that contemporary art theory and criticism are fields in crisis. Indeed, worse than that, he declares an 'emergency' situation for the discipline.[15]

While much more can be said about dominant approaches to responding to or writing about museums (particularly keeping in mind that the museums/culture wars context I am thinking about here relate to a predominantly Australian social history museum context, while Foster's focus is on 'global' art museums and practices), contemporary scholarship has typically emphasized the utility/exceptionalism dichotomy. In its argument predominantly for utility (possibly as a result of the backlash against cultural exceptionalism that became evident through the culture wars), this approach sidelines any discussion about crisis and extends rather than questions the academic assumptions of the discipline, which are, through this process, sustained rather than challenged. This means that scholars have typically focused on writing about how museums respond to crisis rather than examining the agency and role of critical writing in reflecting on crisis or in reproducing the conditions of crisis in a disciplinary context. Even where museum studies writers claim empathy with or even advocate for social justice agendas, we have struggled to find a language and empathy to prosecute this activism on our own terms; we have not been easily able to embody or activate David Graeber's (2008) argument that 'writing itself is engagement' (in Guyer 2016: 374, 376).[16] I include my own writing as having been challenged by the struggle to find an appropriate language and format for addressing museums critically while also making a case for the social value of their work. This has been a key motivation for writing this book.

Our struggle to undertake what Graeber (2008 in Guyer 2016: 376) calls 'insurgent writing' is due, at least in part, to the fact that there is no tradition of disciplinary self-reflection in museum studies. While the function of the critic – and, by extension, the role of criticism – has long been a subject of discussion in fields such as art, literature, and music, it has not in museum studies.[17] An added complication is the genealogical link of museum studies to cultural studies, which has historically resisted attempts at definition (even as it has also 'borrowed' methods from a range of disciplines) (see Ang 2006; Dewdney, Dibosa and Walsh 2013: 1; Message 2015; also Sørensen and Carman 2009b: 23, who make a similar observation about heritage studies). The lack of a tradition of critical writing in the field – about the field – has meant that there is no platform available for engaged debate about disciplinary debate (or crisis). We write 'about' museums, we engage 'with' them, but we do not typically consider the role that critical writing itself may play as a form of intellectual activism in progressing claims shared by museums or other communities. And while writers and artists, community members, anthropologists, or archaeologists do collaborate with museums, the focus of resulting scholarship is usually on the collaboration itself (some exceptions exist, such as Fraser 2005 and Sandell 2016). When we think about crisis, we do so by asking how museums respond to crisis. We never consider how we, as writers, respond to disciplinary crisis or consider how crisis functions in our disciplinary work or its traditions. We typically like to keep our thoughts clean and well-ordered (maintaining normalized disciplinary boundaries and practices), meaning that we have rarely, if ever, tested the limits of criticism in either disciplinary or political contexts (a practice that is critiqued in other disciplinary contexts, Felski 2016).

Crisis . . . what else?[18]

The term 'crisis' pervades debates about the current state of the humanities and social sciences and points to the continued relevance of these academic disciplines for contemporary life and the decision-making frameworks that regulate society, particularly in the postwar period.[19] Favored by culture warriors in the early twenty-first century debates about art, museums, and political interference, the use of the term 'crisis' has escalated to become a ubiquitous feature of political commentary and the critical art press alike, as well as university programs.[20] In an everyday media-saturated world context, crisis is used to explain a crucial or decisive point or situation, an historical conjuncture, or a turning point; it can describe an unstable situation in cultural, political, social, economic, or military affairs, particularly where the situation or event includes the threat or reality of an impending change. It is usually contrasted with both 'emergency' (a situation that poses an immediate risk and that requires urgent attention – such as a cardiac arrest) and 'critique', which is often articulated as a process of reflection or analysis that occurs after a crisis has been resolved. While a crisis can develop into an emergency, it is typically not in itself considered to be acute and can refer to 'an ongoing state of affairs' (Roitman 2012).

Everyday vernacular and academic debates demonstrate that crisis does not always or necessarily result in 'forward' progress or a paradigm shift, as is sometimes thought (Ang 2006). Earlier processes of crisis/critique/ resolution or crisis/resolution/critique worked relative to understandings about what a life without crisis looked like. A life without crisis would typically be perceived as a 'good life', and although the good life genre has been widely critiqued as imaginary (Ahmed 2010; Berlant 2011), it has offered, nonetheless, a constant signifier of normalcy that could be evoked in order to define what crisis is not. Yet the good life fantasy has been critiqued more today than in previous generations, meaning that where crisis exists today, in a world characterized as 'post'-postmodern, there is nothing to compare it to, such that 'crisis' and 'emergency' become more closely related, if not interchangeable terms, as well as the norm rather than an exception to the norm. This situation means that while our experience and expectations of what crisis is might feel heightened, it has also become normalized. It is both a constant and ordinary feature of the present and 'an omnipresent sign in almost all forms of narrative today; it is mobilized as the defining category of our contemporary situation' (Roitman 2012). In other words, we experience crisis as both an ordinary and defining (exceptional) feature of the present.

To demonstrate the extent to which understandings of crisis and normalcy have changed in a generation, anthropologist Janet Roitman (2012) compares Martin Luther King, Jr.'s 1963 'I Have a Dream' speech (the same one I discussed in Chapter 1 via Beck's appropriation of it) with a 2009 speech by Obama (that drew heavily on the language of hope, which I also analyzed in that same chapter). In a passage that shows the political utility of crisis as well as its normalization, Roitman explains:

> On August 28, 1963, Martin Luther King, Jr. mounted the steps of the Lincoln Memorial to deliver a speech entitled 'Normalcy, Never Again.' That day, however, Martin Luther King, Jr. deviated from the 'Normalcy' text to improvise what is now known as the 'I Have A Dream' speech. On January 20, 2009, the day after [Martin] Luther King's birthday, and once having being sworn in as the forty-fourth President of the United States, Barack Obama, deeply conscious of King's legacy and his dream on the Washington Mall, defined contemporary American history in terms of crisis: 'We are in the midst of crisis'. Like King's 'normalcy,' Obama's crisis is used to characterize a moment in history so as to mark off a new age, or a 'journey.' This

journey, defined by Obama in terms of 'struggle' and 'sacrifice,' is historical insofar as it pertains to an economic and political conjuncture.

Vernacular and academic uses of 'crisis' both show that the term has become normalized as a constant and ordinary feature of the present, meaning that there is no longer a plausible alternative. There is, as Martin Luther King, Jr. and Obama both stated, no other 'normal' (and no good life). The main distinction between scholarly and everyday understandings of the term 'crisis' is that academics are more likely to speak of crisis as being a means of action (or a call to arms) rather than a condition (of passivity, chaos, or hopelessness) that requires change – as per Obama's calls for 'hope'. Rather than using crisis to refer primarily to an historical juncture, scholars such as Roitman seek to understand 'the ways that crisis becomes an imperative, or a device for understanding how to act effectively in situations that belie, for the actors, a sense of possibility' (Mbembe and Roitman 1995 in Roitman 2012). In other words, they examine the academic or intellectual political utility of the term for a variety of purposes, including improving understanding about 'the kinds of work the term crisis is or is not doing in the construction of narrative forms' (Roitman 2012).

For a more popularly engaged writer such as Solnit, the critical engagement with crisis is motivated by an attempt to generate an activism (and art) that will 'make a world in which people are producers of meaning, not consumers' (Solnit 2016a: 100). Roitman and Solnit share a commitment to activating (rather than responding to or observing) crisis that is consistent with Luhmann's claim that '[t]he secret of alternative movements is that they cannot offer any alternatives' (Luhmann 1990: 141). This means, of course, that effective activism can no longer rely on the outdated language of 'us' or 'them'. The secret, thus, is not that there is no purpose in activism but that activism needs to recognize the structures within which it operates in order to effect change through modes that are not simply oppositional. This is where the tactics of disobedience, transgression, and dirty thinking come into play and is why understanding crisis as a 'a device for understanding how to act' (Roitman 2012) rather than as a symptom or condition of the status quo is crucial. This project is Foucauldian, because, as Roitman explains:

> For Foucault, crisis signifies a discursive impasse and the potential for a new form of historical subject. . . . [C]risis is productive; it is the means to transgress and is necessary for change or transformation. In keeping with this, because reason has no end other than itself, the decisive duty of critique is essentially to produce crisis – to engage in the

permanent critique of one's self, to be in critical relation to normative life is a form of ethics and a virtue.

(Foucault 1997: 303–19 and Foucault 1985 in Roitman 2012)

The intellectual activism advocated by *The Disobedient Museum: Writing at the Edge* follows this approach. I argue that we need to recognize crisis (within the discipline as well as across the social/political world) as having a fundamentally cognate rather than causal link to critique (Koselleck 1959 in Roitman 2012). Instead of trying to overcome crisis or seeking to recover an 'alternative' norm (practice, discourse, episteme, or institution), our job is to articulate and draw attention to the possibilities of the practice of crisis. We can only do this by identifying crisis as a process of dirty thinking, as disciplinary borderwork that tests the limits of what is acceptable or intelligible within disciplinary and social/political contexts. Rather than seeking the reconstitution of some kind of order (promised via ideologies of a good life), the practice of crisis serves 'the practice of unveiling latencies' by transcending or transgressing oppositions and dichotomies. In other words, although crisis can be used to explain a dystopian status quo (pace the popular media examples discussed at the start of this chapter), the term itself serves as a constant reminder that current frameworks of meaning production can be internally critiqued and challenged. It is the purpose of this book to identify approaches that might be used in the service of such critique. This task requires building a flexible and inclusive conceptual framework that can provide an approach and (paradoxically) a 'tradition' of critique within the discipline of museum studies, as well as demonstrating ways in which this approach can be used for the purposes of social activism as per the calls by cultural, curatorial, and other museum activists.

Notes

1 The need for methods of criticality has been registered in cognate fields such as heritage studies (Sørensen and Carman 2009b), as well as by researchers in museum studies, about which Fiona Cameron and Conal McCarthy (2015: 2) have argued 'the now-classic postcolonial critique of colonial museums and collecting is near exhaustion, and scholarship requires fresh frameworks and approaches in order to move beyond a reductionist analysis of this topic and to open up new angles on the two-way encounter of coloniser and colonised, objects and subjects, human and non-human'. Dewdney, Dibosa and Walsh (2013: 12–13) have argued that however important and influential the approaches of Bourdieu, Foucault and the postcolonial critique have been in the formation of museum studies, 'under the conditions of hypermodernity their explanatory power over the museum has now reached its limit. Newer forms of critical knowledge now need to build upon that legacy'.

2 I similarly accept the full diversity of forms and practices that the term 'writing' covers. While I am principally concerned with academic forums for writing in this book, there is great potential for reflective work by nonacademic and non-text-based genres of writing that can be included here.

3 Keeping in mind that discrete disciplines are not unitary or even homogeneous (Whitehead 2009).

4 Per Judah (2016):

> Changing your Facebook status to reflect the cause *du jour* may well suggest that you are engaged with current affairs and possibly even a lovely human being, but it does not make you an activist (or even an '/activist'). It's notable that the most long-term, politically engaged artists we've spoken to this year have tended to reject the term for themselves, instead reserving it for those who make activism their life's work.

5 The politicization of the mainstream by activist interests is not to be confused with what Stuart Hall (2006 quoted in Dewdney, Dibosa and Walsh 2013: 2) called 'the tricky' situation of 'ambivalent mainstreaming' where people become represented in museums or similar groups as 'acceptable insiders but intellectual outsiders' (in the case, for example, of the apparent inclusion of black British art as represented in New Labour cultural policy priorities), or what Dewdney, Dibosa and Walsh (2013: 2) refer to as museum audiences who are simultaneously represented as 'cultural migrants and internal exiles'.

6 Trends toward greater inclusion and collaboration are widely apparent in national museums conceived and built in the last 20 years and have been the specific focus of attempts to represent the trauma of genocide in museums based on human rights, including Holocaust museums (Macdonald 2008) and identity-based museums such as the National Museum of the American Indian and the National Museum of African American History and Culture (Message 2014), as well as the museums and heritage sites affiliated with the International Coalition of Sites of Conscience.

7 As indeed, some museum professionals and commentators are also starting to do: 'The fallacy of museums as "safe" and "neutral" spaces, particularly for all their employees, has to end. This has never been true' (tweeted @adriannerussell on November 21, 2016, at https://twitter.com/adriannerussell/status/800723797707984897).

8 Dirty thinking also 'seeks to be aware of and avoid the equally problematic trend within postmodernist writing to advance a notion of theory that is insufficiently connected to praxis and a grasp of the social world as a totality' (Ulin 1991: 63, 82).

9 It takes as a guiding motivation Foucault's project to 'respect . . . differences' (Foucault 1973b: xii quoted in Best and Kellner 1991). According to Best and Kellner, this imperative informs Foucault's:

> historical approach, perspectives on society, and political positions and takes numerous forms: a historical methodology which attempts to grasp the specificity and discontinuity of discourses, a rethinking of power as diffused throughout multiple social sites, a redefinition of the 'general intellectual' as a 'specific intellectual', and a critique of global and totalizing modes of thought. Foucault analyzes modernity from various perspectives on modern discourses and institutions.

10 Ang (2006: 183–4) suggests that when asked of cultural studies, these questions reveal 'an ongoing sense of crisis, a general apprehensiveness over the question

whether cultural studies is able to live up to its own self-declared aspirations, both intellectually and politically'.

11 The activism of culture has a long history and, even if we take 1968 as a convenient starting point, includes artists' books, political posters, street art, and avant-garde academic journals, which have all experimented with critical ways of theorizing cultural production in complex social times. The number of museum projects (some based in museums, others not) that are notable today for their attempts to reimagine a new, politically engaged and affective radical museology is growing. These include institutionally affiliated projects such as the Victoria and Albert Museum's *Disobedient Objects* exhibition (www.vam.ac.uk/content/exhibitions/disobedient-objects), non-government-affiliated projects such as the European Disobedience Archive project (www.disobediencearchive.org), and the punk museology project (www.punkmuseology.com). Many independent museum and archive spaces have been collecting radical histories for decades. Examples of these institutions, including the much more recently established Interference Archive (http://interferencearchive.org), in New York, also contribute to this process. A third 'category' of activism in this field is the museum and archive-like projects run under the auspices of protest groups themselves. Examples include the Occupy Archives and Occupy Museums groups of 2011–2012 (precursors of the J20 Art Strike). Beyond these bespoke and event- – or cause- – focused projects, many national and large public museums have, since the culture wars period at least, also expressed a commitment to social justice activism, and the narratives of protest and reform are becoming increasing features of what I have elsewhere (Message 2014) called 'agenda-museums', such as the National Museum of the American Indian and the National Museum of African American History and Culture.

12 A possible exception is the new museology's response to the culture and history wars through the 1990s and 2000s in Western settler societies such as the United States, Canada, New Zealand, and Australia (see Luke 2002; Message 2006). However, the history wars were focused on the writing of history as the construction of historical fact, and what was contested was the history that was written by historians and represented in museums. Contributions by museum scholars to these debates offer early forms of engagement rather than the continuation of a reflective tradition in museum studies of writing about controversy. There is certainly overlap with historical approaches to writing about crisis, but examples at this time typically demonstrated concerns related to 'new' forms of history writing and a reframing of that canon in relation to dominant ideologies and imaginaries of a unified nationhood (one Australian example is Macintyre and Clark 2003).

13 This section draws on the title of Foster (2015), which is drawn from Bertolt Brecht's statement: 'Don't start with the good old days, but the bad new ones'.

14 I have not been able to do justice in this short book to the critical reflection that has, in turn, occurred in response to the phenomenon of institutional critique in art museums and art theory/criticism. This is indicated by Whitehead's (2009: 24) observation that 'bought-in critique by artists stands in for more sustained and transparent self-critique on the part of museum workers concerning the responsibilities of knowledge construction, which has yet to happen'. This critique implicitly suggests that the now familiar forms of this work (in Fred Wilson's *Mining the Museum* style of museological intervention) has had much less of an impact than has been claimed. It also suggests a maintenance

of rather than challenge to the traditional effect of aesthetic isolation from day-to-day political discourses and effects. If this is the case, the interventions do not realize the increasingly commonly stated expectation that they are diverse, representative, and 'democratic'. See Wilson (2010) and Dewdney, Dibosa and Walsh (2013: 90–1).

15 Foster's assessment that this period of criticality and the associated engagement of art museums and art theory/criticism with political culture was short-lived combines with the argument that the 'new art history' (Rees and Borzello 1986) had only a momentary effect on canonical forms of art historical writing to suggest that this field may be in a continuous form of disrepair or crisis (Jõekalda 2013). Rather than making art history a poor model for museum studies to learn from, it nonetheless remains a cognate dialogical field from which to draw comparisons, contrasts, and possibly alliances. The impact of the 'new' art history can be compared with the enduring influence of the 'history from below' approach championed by British cultural historian Raphael Samuel, a scholar noted for his role in establishing the History Workshop movement, which aimed to involve ordinary people as both subjects and prac-titioners of history (and which was influential on the field of heritage studies that also developed through this period). See Fielding (2007) and Gentry (2015, and Samuel (1994)) for Samuel's impact on the cognate field of heritage stud-ies. Also note that Samuel's approach to history writing influenced Greg Den-ing, whose work is addressed in Chapter 3 as offering a clear model for writing about museums.

16 Graeber is an anthropologist and anarchist activist who played a key role in the formation of the Occupy movement. He has sometimes been credited with hav-ing coined the slogan 'We are the 99%' (Jeffries 2015).

17 This can be understood to an extent as a definitional problem, although as with some of our cognate fields, we lack clear borders/parameters to begin the pro-cess of defining what museum criticism is or should be. For example, Pezzini (2015: 6) argues:

> Art history is a discipline in fieri, still in search of a definition, and an investigation into the art press reveals the inception of this disorientation as well as a developing quest for terminology and clarification. For instance, there still exists an abiding and deep-seated tension between definitions of 'art criticism' and 'art history,' as is evident by the prevalence of the recent term, 'art writing'.

This statement is also relevant to museum studies, as an interdisciplinary field still in flux and in search of a definition but also torn by its ties to cultural stud-ies, in which such definitional determinism is unwanted.

18 I have borrowed this title from a festival of street art held in Athens in 2013 of the same name. Organized by GA Art+Events Mgmt, the Athens School of Fine Arts, and the Municipality of Nikaia, the festival explored the critical potential of street art in the context of the Greek financial crisis; however, it attracted controversy for excluding any Greek artists, despite the proliferation of street art by local artists in Athens and other Greek cities. For acute visual commentary about the controversy, see http://bleeps.gr/main/outdoor/crisis-what-else-9/

19 In an academic context, 'crisis texts' have become the stuff of a 'vast' and 'veri-table industry' (Roitman 2012).

20 Although 'crisis' is not listed in the 13 most overused words referred to at the outset of this chapter, it arguably could be. In terms of cultural studies, for instance, Ang (2006: 184) has observed that:

> this persistent sense of crisis – which in fact can be a productive force in itself – is compounded by cultural studies' self-declared claim to be a politically informed intellectual practice. But what does 'political' mean here? In which ways can cultural studies, as a predominantly academic practice, have a political impact or effect?

3   Writing resistance

Figure 3.1 Contested freedoms: Independent protester on Independence Avenue boundary between Restoring Honor rally and Reclaim the Dream march, Washington, D.C., August 28, 2010

Photograph by Kylie Message.

How to write about museums

Critique is a process that demands engagement with contemporary circumstances, a capacity to act, and an engagement with place and context. It requires a readiness to move and to be moved. My conception of critique is similar to the process of engaged research that Amanda Third examines. She cites a researcher (known as interviewee E) who describes the process of active research as being 'all in the *timing*. You have to be on guard, always ready to intervene, to push the boundaries, to throw out a challenge. It is this capacity to react – almost instinctually but with the full force of what you know activated in the moment – that is the mark of the engaged researcher' (E quoted in Third 2016: 107).

Understanding critique as a form of engaged research is particularly important for writing about museums, in which the locale is often both the subject and the site of research and writing. I investigate this approach by opening this chapter with a consideration of review writing, which can offer one model for engaged forms of writing about museums, particularly case-study based approaches. Review writing evidences an encounter with an object and its context, as well as the discursive frames through which the review is written. It is grounded in place (the museum and the site occupied by the writer), as well as a disciplinary tradition – both of which attribute meaning to the review.

Review writing – of books, exhibitions, or other products, events, or experiences – is also a process of interpretation, commentary, and critique that has made a significant contribution to shaping and challenging disciplines within the humanities over a great many decades. However, it tends to be an activity that is uncelebrated in a contemporary context, perhaps because it is ranked as a low-importance type of publication by university measures and assessment of outputs or perhaps as an outcome of the growth of interdisciplinary fields where there is a limited tradition of critique, where the relationship of the process of critique to the activity of review writing is not clear and thus undervalued (Post 2009: 769). Foster has argued that the practices of critical writing have languished as a result of the politics of the culture wars and the associated 'turn' within humanities disciplines through the 1990s and 2000s to embrace culture and cultural and community-based forms of engaged research practice. The so-called cultural turn was an inclusive and democratic one that was perceived by conservative power brokers as a threat to dominant representations of knowledge and power. The turn toward culture and the conditions of knowledge production and exchange also signaled a rejection of the so-called linguistic turn (and its attendant poststructuralist/postmodern tendency to interpret the world as a text) that had characterized the latter half of the twentieth century.

The cultural turn of the 1990s represented an important move toward refocusing our work as writers and thinkers on impacts – of the impact, for example, of text on the world and vice versa (among other relationships). It also drew attention to research and writing (representation) as a form of exchange, negotiation, and ultimately a play of power relations associated with authority. While this shift resulted for the most part in the recognition of the need for engagement, interaction, and discussion about the value of research itself (and for whom), interest in the genre of review writing *as* critique, at least in the disciplines I am most familiar with, may have been diminished. This has meant, in the context of art criticism associated with the postmodern journal *October*, for example, that 'the path-breaking essays' of Rosalind Krauss, Douglas Crimp, and Craig Owens of 1979–1980 are yet to be 'properly documented' and that as a consequence there has been less than widespread recognition of the journal's 'considerably significant role in setting the terms and conditions through which a critical postmodernism would take hold in the art world' in the years that followed (Bowman 2015: 118). While Matthew Bowman's concern is with preserving the legacy of individual intellectuals, I think a more important point is that in having lost some of our mechanisms – however flawed – to write critique, we have suppressed some elements of the past about which we should be reflecting upon critically (as object of critique), as well as one framework through which we might be able to think about how to do this.

Despite the shortcomings of adopting a purely poststructuralist/postmodern approach to explaining the world, I have often found review writing to be productive – not just as a way to keep up with current literature but as an impetus to think critically about how my own work engages with and is located within the context of the broader field that the review and book or exhibit being reviewed contribute to shape. I have approached review writing as a reflexive writing process that has been as much about understanding and applying a critical lens to my own work as it is to engaging in this same manner with the work being reviewed. Beyond the value this exercise has offered to my own work, reflective forms of writing are consistent with descriptions of 'affective' and disruptive writing, as processes of articulation that help put dirty thinking into words and that are central to the process of exploring and articulating the disobedient museum project and its contribution to intellectual activism.[1]

Rethinking the process of review is a timely activity in terms of understanding what critique might look like today, in the context of current disciplinary approaches as well as a contemporary experience marked by increasing political activism. Attempts to return to and reactivate work that had been taking place well before and alongside the linguistic turn and its 'attendant social constructionisms' (Seigworth and Gregg 2010: 7) might also offer the conditions by which new or renewed ways for articulating experience might occur. Indeed, Bowman's task was to make a similar case for reassessing the relationship between the critical writing at the heart of *October* and disciplinary (theoretical) and artistic development.[2] Arguing

that 'much of our contemporary sense of what comprises postmodernism for the visual arts is fundamentally rooted in the intellectual positions
advanced by *October* in 1976–1981' (Bowman 2015: 117), he remains
aware of the dangers of recuperation, which he seeks to avoid by employing
an 'engaged' framework of affect and interaction (rather than authority) that
he attributes to the reflexive process of art critic Craig Owens. In describing Owens's refusal of dichotomous terminology, Bowman says, 'Against
this privileging of the art critic and the reduction of art to the pre-reflexive,
Owens clearly resituates his own practice'. The shift that is outlined by
Bowman's work follows Owens's reflections of his earlier publications to
demonstrate 'a methodological shift in academic art history, from an essentially object-based study to a broader investigation of network' (Pezzini
2015: 6) and relationships. The 'split between critic and artist, then, had
been compromised', says Owens, meaning that 'we were writing not necessarily about these critical and opposition practices but alongside them.
There was an exchange there, and one's criticism was conducting the same
work in a different arena and in a different way'. Bowman (2015: 124)
articulates Owen's process of borderwork to argue:

> Understanding art criticism in this manner compels us to reject any
> conception that posits criticism as merely commentary, reportage,
> description, or simply judgment – that is to say, as reception. Instead,
> we must also attend to its productive dimensions, theorizing and histo-
> ricizing how art and its criticism are necessarily imbricated.

Museum revolutions

In order to think about how a reflective, exchange-based approach to writing about museums – where, in this case, my attention is on 'writing about'
rather than the 'museum' as subject – can work and what it might look like,
I start this chapter by revisiting a review I wrote several years ago about a
book called *Museum Revolutions: How Museums Change and Are Changed*
(Knell, MacLeod and Watson 2007a), which is an edited volume representative of approaches used to write about museums at that time.[3] While my
reflection might prima facie provide a benchmark to identify changes in the
practice of writing about museums in the decade since its publication, I am
less concerned with measuring 'progress' than I am focused on understanding how our work as writers both influences and is impacted by institutional
and social transformation, as well as disciplinary trends, because, as Foster
(2015: 2) has noted, terminology is a collective project. Nonetheless, there
has been an increase in the use in museum scholarship in recent years of

seemingly uncompromising oppositional words such as 'revolution', 'radical', and 'anti-' in the context of museum practice and writing, an approach I seek to counteract rather than adopt by instead returning to the unfashionable review's emphasis on critical writing as a process of borderwork that has become increasingly evident as a key element of the disobedient museum concept/process (hence the subtitle of this book: *Writing at the Edge*).

My approach, indicated from the outset of the book – 'This is not a protest. This is a process' (Gledhill 2012: 342) – is influenced by practices by Michel de Certeau (1984) and other theorists who have explored the unseen and informal moments of urban life. 'Rather than remaining within the field of a discourse that upholds its privilege by inverting its content (speaking of catastrophe and no longer of progress)', urges de Certeau (1984: 96), 'one can try another path or another approach'. This process does not demand that we look elsewhere or 'outside' (which is, as I established in Chapter 2, impossible). It means identifying the spaces and practices of alterity within our daily lives and in the systems and structures of experience and oppression. De Certeau (1984) provides as an example of a potentially subversive action the exercise of walking, as a pedestrian movement that forms one the 'real systems whose existence in fact makes up the city' where the meaning created by the walker does not always align with or respect the marked pathways and structures of organization and government regulation that these represent. My secondary goal with prosecuting a performance, politics, and practice of borderwork in this chapter – the disobedient museum project sits across boundaries and, like the walker who takes her or his own actions, thereby rejects attempts at categorization – is to demonstrate the related point made by Fraser and others that using a terminology of opposition is not appropriate to a situation where an inside/outside dichotomy no longer exists. As Fraser (2005) comments:

> With each attempt to evade the limits of institutional determination, to embrace an outside, to redefine art or reintegrate it into everyday life, to reach 'everyday' people and work in the 'real' world, we expand our frame and bring more of the world into it. But we never escape it. . . . that frame has also been transformed in the process.

My decision to approach this chapter by reflecting on a previous review about a specific book is due more to the circumstances of my engagement with it than with the book itself. I started reading *Museum Revolutions* (Knell, MacLeod and Watson 2007a) at the end of the university teaching term, as I was wrapping up tasks associated with a graduate course that familiarized students with the techniques scholars use to design and undertake empirical and theoretical research. The course challenged students to rehearse and evaluate a range of interdisciplinary approaches to humanities research (from the perspectives of critical literary theory, anthropology, art criticism, law, archaeology and environmental studies, museum and cultural studies, history, and criminology). Students came from a diverse range of fields, although most were interested in exploring what this pluralistic and polyglot thing called 'interdisciplinary research' is and how it might be adopted into their own research design and projects.

Although I am not sure that we talk about interdisciplinarity in quite the same way now, it remains in its most pragmatic form a practice and process of combining and adapting existing methods to develop new or alternative approaches to our research problems and questions, which may themselves be new or old or repurposed or revisited.[4] Being interdisciplinary is not about casually incorporating elements in a pick-and-mix style, and it requires engaging with a field in a way that is discursively defensible.[5] An interdisciplinary researcher is cognizant of the practices of multiple fields and can confidently employ certain tools, strategies, and approaches on the grounds that they are best suited to their subject matter or because they might provide a way in which to extend or challenge the normalized boundaries of the discipline with which the researcher primarily identifies and is embedded and to which they seek to contribute. It often extends from a desire to a find a way to negate the situation of being 'trapped' in a field by actively aiming to extend, challenge, and perhaps redefine the field's parameters, processes, and even vocabularies. It is also about 'feeling one's way', even where experience does not appear to match the methodological tool kits that have been provided by our usual disciplinary frameworks (as my referencing of art criticism/theory may demonstrate). In their attempt to map this space of 'feeling' by way of affect theory, which is, like cultural studies and museum studies an interdisciplinary area with somewhat indeterminate boundaries, Gregory J. Seigworth and Melissa Gregg described early encounters with theories of affect in terms of a trial-and-error process of 'methodological and conceptual free fall' (2010: 4). 'Because affect emerges out of muddy, unmediated relatedness and not in some dialectical reconciliation of cleanly oppositional elements or primary units', argue Seigworth and Gregg (2010: 4), 'it makes easy compartmentalisms give way to thresholds and tensions, blends and blurs' (see also Witcomb 2015b for discussion of affect in the museological context).

While some experiences and frameworks will match up and others will not, researchers are often drawn to interdisciplinary research for 'tactical' reasons (Third 2016). Interdisciplinary work can, for example, be a requirement for researchers seeking to develop inclusive collaborative working relationships across theoretical and practical – as well as disciplinary – fields. This kind of 'engaged' research is primarily concerned with 'fostering an active dialogue within a "community" of practice' (Wenger 2000) that plays 'a powerful pedagogic role for research, policy, and practice alike' (Third

2016: 94).[6] An accompanying motivation has been explained by historian and anthropologist Greg Dening (1998, 2000), who argued that interdisciplinary work can lead to new ways of understanding past events and peoples. Despite sharing some similarities with Foucault's attention to genealogy, Dening promoted a 'reflective' approach to scholarly activity (whereby individual researchers adopt a self-conscious and empirical approach to their own scholarly activity) and expressed caution about theoretically informed 'reflexive' approaches that aim to create challenging critiques of generalized disciplinary paradigms. Unpacking his motivations for experimenting with what was at the time a different kind of history-work, Dening explained:

> I wanted to write history of the encounters between intruding settler societies and native first peoples in Oceania, the Australian-Pacific region. I wanted to see what the strangers saw from their ships or their forts or their camps or their mission stations. More importantly, I wanted to see what they didn't see. For that I thought I needed a reading skill that I didn't have. It was anthropology, I thought. I didn't want to become an anthropologist. I wanted the skills of an anthropologist to translate and hear the silences of another culture. . . . I never really wanted to contribute to the discourse of anthropology. I did want to contribute to the discourse of history.
>
> (Dening 2000: 211)[7]

Borderwork

In this chapter I move from the metaphor of the encounter to outline the concept of borderwork, before exploring the consequent idea that disciplinary borders (like the museums that are often identified as contact zones) are constantly involved in processes of change, albeit at varying speeds and rates (evidence that, as Fraser 2005 argues, our discursive 'frame has also been transformed in the process' of engagement). A focus on affective writing as a process of encounter, borderwork, and fundamentally engagement underpins this trajectory. It is a process that will be explored subsequently throughout this chapter but that is relevant to introduce here for the way it simultaneously builds on and contrasts with Dening's statement because, although Dening was a famously affective writer, there are few signs of this proclivity in the preceding passage, which is unusual for its restrained tone and which can be understood as being at pains to demonstrate that remaining too loyal to any singular discipline is inadequate to access cross-cultural ways of learning, listening, and perhaps knowing. I like to think that Dening (2000) was trying to argue that in order for researchers to be properly engaged and for writers to be affective, they need to fully understand the practices, benefits, limitations, and rough edges of the discipline within which they are working before they can jump into the messy, experiential, and highly situated dimensions that a critical and affective approach can create for reading and writing alike. Michael Richardson (2015) explains:

> The embodied self needs to be understood not solely in terms of its relations with the text, but its multitude of contingent and always-changing relation to texts, media, spaces, knowledges, histories, geographies. In short, that judgment of a text be suspended in favour of its generative possibilities (Abel 2007). Affect offers one possibility of fulfilling Foucault's dream of 'a kind of criticism that would try not to judge but to bring an oeuvre, a book, a sentence, an idea to life' (1997: 323). Yet what might this criticism beyond judgment entail? Woven into this question is the mode of critical writing called for by affect, how such critique might take objects as they are (Muecke 2012), and how both reading and writing are enfolded by the critiquing, embodied self.

Rather than being exclusive or nondialogical concepts, my shift from a discussion about the limitations of disciplinarity (Dening 2000) to the promises of affect theory (Richardson 2015; Seigworth and Gregg 2010; Third 2016) is not designed to privilege one term or approach over the other but to show that both are necessary for any attempt to understand contemporary and historical experiences. Indeed, each term – disciplinarity and affect theory – are useful to keep in dialogue because they can be used to hold accountable the approaches employed by the other. In other words, these terms are not bound by dichotomies around structuralism/affect or otherwise and have been included here to demonstrate the extent to which each in fact rely on the other. It also demonstrates the extent to which I continue to be inspired by the work of scholars who seek primarily to make a contribution to fields other than museum studies, particularly those working at the intersection of sociology, anthropology, and cultural studies, which has been described by Graeme Turner as 'a kind of academic *lingua franca* for the new humanities, a common theoretical and methodological language which may enable those disciplines engaged in cultural research to work with each other' (Turner 2012: 12 in Third 2016).

Other work that continues to be influential on my own approach to writing about museums includes the less formal genres of book reviews, commentaries, and working papers, which offer platforms for experimentation for some writers. Examples include work already cited here – Dening's book review (2000), which explores interdisciplinary 'encounters', Fraser's (2005) reflection essay on institutional critique – as well as a working paper by anthropologist Marilyn Strathern concerning boundary disciplines, and James Clifford's 2007 review, 'Quai Branly in Process.' These texts have a particular resonance because museums are likewise about encounters, exchanges, and the establishment and maintenance, as well as transgression of boundaries that are discursive as well as physical/experiential. An editorial by critical theorist Lauren Berlant has been influential for its approach to probing the 'case' – that is, the standard unit in law, medicine, psychoanalysis, the humanities, the sciences, and popular culture – to ask what makes a case ordinary, easily dealt with, or forgettable? What makes some but not all cases effective as challenges to the way ordinary life or institutional systems usually proceed? Critically, Berlant (2007: 664) explained in this (pre-*Cruel Optimism*) work that, as a genre, the case 'hovers about the singular, the general, and the normative' but can also incite an opening, an altered way of feeling things out, of falling out of line. The case study approach advocated by Berlant (2007) is a political exercise that has a close affiliation with the tactical work described by Michel de Certeau in *The Practice of Everyday Life*. 'A tactic operates in isolated actions, blow by blow', he says:

> it takes advantage of 'opportunities' and depends on them, being without any base where it could stockpile its winnings, build up its own position, and plan raids. What it wins it cannot keep. This nowhere gives a tactic mobility, to be sure, but a mobility that must accept the chance offerings of the moment, and seize on the wing of possibilities that offer themselves at any given moment.
>
> (de Certeau 1984: 36–7)

Tactics occur within and against the totalizing organizational strategic social/political structures upon which 'political, economic, and scientific rationality has been constructed' (de Certeau 1984: xix). They 'do not obey the law of the place, for they are not defined or identified by it', and whereas strategies, aligned with structural governmental power, are able to 'produce, tabulate, and impose these spaces' of authority, tactics can only use, reuse, manipulate, disrupt, and divert these spaces (de Certeau 1984: 29, 30). They are aligned with everyday practices that we use – shortcuts and 'knowing how to get away with things' (de Certeau 1984: xix) – and that constitute small-scale forms of protest or disruption in the space of the everyday – which is the realm of both the museum *and* the museum-like experience – as well as the language and discursive forms that we use to represent, explain, and make sense of these experiences. De Certeau explains that, although tactical movements or articulations are:

[c]omposed with the vocabularies of established languages (those of television, newspapers, supermarkets, or museum sequences) and although they remain subordinated to the prescribed syntactical forms (temporal modes of schedules, paradigmatic orders of spaces, etc.), the trajectory trace out of the ruses of other interests and desires that are neither determined nor captured by the systems in which they develop.

(de Certeau 1984: xviii)

Museum Revolutions extended my interest in disciplinary borderwork and writing at, or from, the edge because, despite having a stated interest in 'the study of the history and theory of museums and disciplinarity' in one chapter (Whitehead 2007: 48), the volume remained for the most bound by an oppositional form of logic. According to the editors of *Museum Revolutions* (Knell, MacLeod and Watson 2007b: xix):

Museums are in revolt. Revolution here then is a process which objectifies a set of values and an imagined past, and then follows a future that in some ways is oppositional and new. Or to put it another way, the museum sees two possible futures, one that reflects the present trajectory and one that can be obtained by reinvention.

This kind of either/or embattled thinking (which presumes an opposition between past and future instead of understanding the relationship between these as a continuum) was relevant in the culture wars context of the day, particularly given the urgent feeling at the time that the arts and culture were being directly targeted for funding cuts on the basis of an ideological position argued by the conservative right that was gaining political and public traction. However the defensive approach reflected the discipline's lack of language for imagining or modeling the kind of future it would like to see for museums.

It is relevant to revisit the volume's editorial statement here because while the political situation and challenges to museums and culture have evolved since the culture wars of the first decade of the early twenty-first century (and practices of protest), the language of opposition has remained the primary discursive form employed by museums and projects such as the 'anti-university'.[8] The confusion in the Carnegie press release discussed in Chapter 1 reveals many of the difficulties associated with identifying effective forms of criticism for museums that are inherently complex and paradoxical spaces. This is accurate for all the reasons it raises, most prominent among them being the funding cuts and ubiquitous challenges to/reinventions of normative discourses of utility and national identity. As the new Iceland Punk Museum in Reykjavik and the broader punk museology project both endeavor to show, museums have evolved alongside the political/social context such that they are required to manage these sometimes conflicting narratives. Conflicting missions can be held by a museum and the governmental or funding agency to which it is accountable, a situation illustrated by the Iceland Punk Museum, about which Gudrun Whitehead explains: 'It's hard to be a punk when working within the confines of government regulations. . . . How do you set up an exhibition on anarchy within the institutional establishment that is the museum?' (Whitehead 2016). In this new, altogether 'other' day (Gellner 1965: 67 in Guyer 2016: 374), straightforward narratives of opposition are not effective because direct opposition implies a wholesale rejection or refusal of a status quo that is incompatible with a process of reflective critique, which demands engagement with the conditions by which the situation/order has been created and is maintained. In agreeing to the terms of the dichotomy by asserting the correctness of one 'side' over the other, this approach withholds the agency that a process of borderwork can insist on, advocate for, or preserve as primary in any process of negotiation.

A different approach might understand 'the future' as being constituted as a continuation of the present as much as a reinvention of it. This approach would identify the ongoing disruptions of crisis as contributing to the 'present trajectory' and recognize lessons learned from such disruptions, including, for example, Beck's subversion of a site and language associated with Martin Luther King, Jr., addressed in Chapter 1. Rather than being a simple inversion of meaning, Beck's process was more akin to de Certeau's theory of tactical reappropriation whereby the everyday users of a street willfully challenge political regulations, order, or official meanings of a space through their shortcuts and other movements. He took a high-profile space that was already contested and used the language of civil rights to claim it for the '99%' (a category that ostensibly was inclusive of *all* Americans, not just the Tea Partyers but those rallying for civil rights in the name of Martin Luther King, Jr.). These examples of subversion – both by Beck (of the national imaginary), and de Certeau's walkers – show that tactics of direct opposition are less effective in a liminal (contested) context than those of measured disobedience, defiance, or even a lack of action or a refusal to move, be defined, or obey. This is a key lesson for museums, which are always already contested sites, as recognized by the editors of *Museum Revolutions*, who, although they did not probe the potential of border zones as spaces for intellectual/disciplinary transgression, claimed in the publisher's blurb: 'While change has been on the museum professional's agenda for twenty years, this book is the first to reveal its complexity and frame it in the context of contemporary museum studies'. In effect, *Museum*

Revolutions (Knell, MacLeod and Watson 2007a) demonstrated the point that although there are no shortage of possible case studies that could be developed around museums that are central to debates about value, the thing that is missing is an understanding and practice about how to write about museums and debate, particularly if writers have the goal of themselves making an activist contribution.

While the majority of this chapter addresses borderwork as a theoretical model usually affiliated with social history and anthropology (and often correlating with national museums), it is relevant to keep in mind its gene-alogical links with the idea of an avant-garde that is always already con-junctural (in that it does not respect boundaries) and 'immanent' (in that it is neither past or future but always in the process of becoming another moment):

> [T]he avant-garde that interests me here is neither *avant* nor rear in these senses; rather, it is immanent in a caustic way. Far from heroic, it does not pretend that it can break absolutely with the old order or found a new one; instead it seeks to trace fractures that already exist within the given order, to pressure them further, even to activate them somehow. Far from defunct, this avant-garde is alive and well today.
>
> (Foster 2015: 4)

All the readings for the course that I read with my class 'around' *Museum Revolutions* (Knell, MacLeod and Watson 2007a) represented interdisciplin-ary humanities research as a kind of borderwork sympathetic to Foster's understanding of the avant-garde, as something that occurs at the edges of disciplines, at the point of friction or messy intersection between discur-sive and materialist investigations, and at the place where discourse among academics, professionals, and the public may occur. The correspondences that emerged between the readings and as a result of class discussions also created new ways of thinking about ongoing questions that were significant for my scholarly work at that time and to which I have find myself return-ing and reflecting. In particular, these questions led to what have become enduring questions for me – about whether museum studies might function as a 'boundary discipline' and to the demand that relationships between museum studies and disciplines including history, anthropology, sociology, and cultural studies be further scrutinized in order to simultaneously iden-tify and analyze the contingent historical conditions of those fields. It has surprised me that, despite the calls made by museum studies for museums to be increasingly political and accountable to social justice agendas, there has not been an equivalent attention to the politics of writing in this field. One pathway for this, which is what I explore here, is revisiting the genre of critique which, despite being accused of being bound to structuralist approaches and restricted by political context, continues to provide one of a limited range of opportunities to engage with writing about culture and political activism in an environment that is not tied to discourses of utility.

Activist writing

The questions and impetus for researching and exploring the politics of writing about museums also point to the ongoing necessity (that is perhaps more acute today) of undertaking a reflective *and* reflexive reassessment of the disciplinary orientation as well as the apparatus and practices of an agile museum studies that might produce new ways to rethink the complex relationships between culture and society in a contemporary as well as an historical context. Again, I think the 'small' forms and 'minor' genres of writing (assessed as unimportant by university-quality measures), including review writing and critique, have a role to play in this on the grounds that, 'as new questions arise about freedom, identity, religion, and related matters, many writers feel compelled not only to capture the social and political issues of their time, but also to use writing to change notions about the world we live in'.[9] This impetus builds on my argument from Chapter 2 that it is relevant to theorize the contemporary in a timely way because crisis (defined as either an action of response *or* as the absence of such an action) needs to be understood as a defining feature of the contemporary condition. It also provides the key rationale for the Museums in Focus series, which has been designed as a short format book series that provides a forum for writers to produce timely and engaged, if experimental, forms of critique. In other words, the series offers a conceptual worksite for writers to test out new ways of writing about urgent contemporary issues, recognizing that crisis is never far from critique (partly because of its disciplinary limitations).

Although it should not be assumed that an engagement with or critique of contemporary concerns is activist by default,[10] it has been associated with an intellectual activism that positions writing (1) as a means to produce knowledge to inform progressive social change, (2) as a means for conducting research that itself involves social change, (3) as a site for progressive strategies of teaching and learning, and finally (4) as an institution whose power relations themselves may be challenged and reconstructed. Central to this activism are attempts to identify a framework or vocabulary that 'reframes the problems from another subject position, one that articulates norms and forms differently' (Rabinow 2012 in Deliss and Keck 2016: 387) – where 'differently' refers to a process that does not denunciate the present from a more authentic position in the past or in the future (consistent with Foster's representation of the avant-garde) or from a more familiar speaking position.

Borderwork as a form of engaged research has been an increasing feature in recent discussions about the role of affective writing in the context of contemporary anthropology (which has, in the Trump era, been addressed by some scholars (Stoller 2017) as a key form of activism) and cultural studies. Speaking from a cultural studies perspective and influenced by de Certeau, Amanda Third (2016) has argued that the academic researcher is a 'tactical agent' who engages in a collaborative process of knowledge production that is grounded in a community of practice peopled by other 'expert citizens' who put forward competing ideas, including those about the impact of this work on knowledge forms. Borderwork in this context is both interdisciplinary and involves collaboration of differently located people across the borders that have traditionally separated institutional and noninstitutional places and communities. In contemporary anthropology (that is, the anthropology of the contemporary), the emphasis has similarly been on a review of recent and past work by Paul Rabinow, who argued for an engaged form of scholarship in which the writer shares the experience of ' "being on the verge" along with our subjects' (Guyer 2016: 373; Rabinow 2007: 12).[11] To understand what this position (as well as perspective) entails, Jane Guyer explains that 'to recognize a "verge" in the first place, one needs to be there, in the weeds and the undergrowth' (Guyer 2016: 376). She says:

> 'The contemporary', as Rabinow applies the term, places everything that is entailed in research into the same frame, 'adjacent' to each other: the objects and their intellectual depiction; the researcher and his/her actions and collaborations; and the temporal frame, in this case, the present not as a timeless 'ethnographic present' but as an unfolding event. To quote him: 'An anthropology of the contemporary faces the challenge of finding a means to remain close to diverse current practices producing knowledge, ethics, and politics, while adopting an attitude of discernment and adjacency in regard to them, thereby providing a space for a more precise and better formulation of contemporary problems and risks (2007: 29). In this orientation, there is no disciplined objectivity and focused observation that hold[s] some dynamics out of the picture.
>
> (Guyer 2016: 373)

Borderwork is consistent with this process because, rather than insisting on separation, it demonstrates adjacencies and contact between terms that all share the same field. This is an important point for showing that while there is, on the one hand, no 'outside', the process of engagement and interaction that occurs across boundaries within this space does, 'of course', mean 'that frame has also been transformed in the process' (Fraser 2005). Christopher Whitehead's (2007) essay in *Museum Revolutions* models one way in which we might start to think about the process of disciplinary reassessment required to consider the practice of activist writing in the context of museum studies, making the point that even where our subject might be historical rather than contemporary, a contingent relationship brings it into contact. This does not mean interpreting past practice through a contemporary lens or according to a presentist set of values but drawing points of contact across temporal boundaries via appropriate dialogical means. To do this, Whitehead examines the emergence of art history and disciplinarity in the nineteenth century in the context of professional decision-making processes occurring at the time. He addresses the contingent historical conditions in which the equivocal relationship between museum practice and the knowledges evoked by museums as public cultural institutions emerged. His chapter sought to reevaluate the contemporary relationship between museum theory and practice and to destabilize the dialectical tension existing between an art history that is 'not satisfactorily reduced to being the "theory" to the museum's "practice" ' – and a museum that rejects any conceptualization of the institution as simply an 'exemplification or application of art history' (Donald Preziosi 2006: 50–1 in Whitehead 2007: 48). In line with his objective to 'push boundaries', Whitehead's approach (2007: 55) was 'to understand what museums collect and display and why and how they do so as a form of boundary work'.

Relational thinking

In contrast to *Museum Revolutions*, which primarily takes the museum as its primary object of study, my interest here is in the discourse of contemporary museum studies, or what, at the time *Museum Revolutions* was published, was referred to as the new museology (also see Message 2006). Building on understandings about 'contemporary' art and culture explored by Rabinow and subsequent theorists, including Terry Smith (2009, 2015) and Claire Bishop (whose approach I address shortly), I am specifically concerned to examine what it might mean to suggest that museum studies functions as what I will, following Strathern, call a 'boundary discipline'. Strathern draws from Corynne McSherry's proposition that a boundary object 'holds different meanings in different social worlds, yet is imbued with enough shared meaning to facilitate its translation across those worlds' (McSherry 2001: 69 cited in Strathern 2004: 45, also see Strathern 2016 for discussion about the ethical considerations and impacts of these translations). This description is analogous to the discourse of reciprocity and continual renegotiation through which James Clifford, following Mary Louise Pratt

(1991, 1992), characterizes the museum as a contact zone. Clifford (1997: 204) suggests that the museum's embodiment of this concept can lead to the 'more democratic' transgression of borders. Both the concepts of the contact zone and the boundary object centralize language and debate as a kind of mediation and/or transaction across disciplinary or other divides and propose that a distinctive social character can emerge within the space. It is notable that Pratt's use of the contact zone concept also developed through a study of linguistics, particularly pidgin and creole languages (Pratt 1991, 1992; see also Kratz and Karp 2006: 27, fn 1). These concepts may similarly be invoked in different ways and through multiple pedagogical contexts. Neither presupposes that the borders they establish will function as enclosures. Speaking about further possible applications of the theme in language that accords with the new museology's account of changes over this period, Strathern (2004: 45) says:

> The contemporary intensification of debate over the relationship between knowledge and the public good, and how creativity can be pressed into productive use (for the nation reconceived as an economy), is coming to characterize a rather different kind of university from that which occupied most of the twentieth century. We might look for new boundary objects. Are *disciplines* being re-created as boundary objects of a kind?

The changes in public culture and institutions discussed by Strathern in terms of universities have likewise contributed to the desire to create a 'different' kind of museum that is aligned with and informed by a museum studies that promotes reflective and reflexive practice (as also documented by various examples throughout *Museum Revolutions*). This practice is often associated with Foucault's rationale and hypothesis for moving from 'traditional' to 'effective' – that is, localized and contingent – depictions where history is understood as 'an ongoing effort (or process) to make, unmake, and remake relations, structures, and unity (on top of differences)' (Grossberg 2006: 4; Foucault 1977). Beth Lord's essay in *Museum Revolutions* explores the impetus for employing a reflective, 'effective' genealogical approach in relation to museum exhibitions that reproduce the aesthetic (object-based) versus anthropological (narrative-driven) dichotomy. Following Foucault, Lord asserts that this oppositional logic can be destabilized if it is recognized that:

> The historical object is no longer a tool of memory, but a way of developing and opening up what makes us what we are. In this way, history becomes genealogy. We no longer treat the past as a total object that is other than us, but that which is contained in multiple, changing ways

in what we are. We can understand our present in a new way, through opening up new historical series as its conditions of possibility.

(Lord 2007: 365)

Although she is concerned in this instance with the material museum object, Lord's call for relational thinking can also be applied to the 'object' conceived as museum studies.[12] Her attention to genealogy as a methodology (rather than as an outcome) means that her essay illustrates the sometimes causal intersections that can occur between borderwork, genealogy, and revolution. 'How will museums think about the relations between objects, concepts and history in the twenty-first century?' she asks before responding with her proposition that 'a new way to think about how the object is related to concepts' is needed (Lord 2007: 355, 356).

Lord's attempt to show that the new museology's attention to reflective and reflexive scholarship influences the way in which this genealogy is produced has clear implications for the discourse of museum studies as well as the museum profession. It is globally and widely apparent that museums developed in the last 30 years or so – themselves conscious of the challenges, constraints, and possibilities outlined by this and the other chapters – are endeavoring to produce relational and 'affective' approaches toward collections management, exhibition development, and museum design and that they are also contributing to the ongoing development of the discipline (as also explored in the context of Whitehead's historical study). This interplay is evident, for example, in relation to founding director of the National Museum of the American Indian, Richard West's (2000: 7) contention that, upon opening, the museum would be a 'radically different' and increasingly democratic museum. We can also see it in Clifford's response to the Musée du quai Branly, published soon after that museum opened in Paris in 2006, in which he suggested that the museum might 'present intriguing possibilities for something different' (Clifford 2007: 14). Acknowledging the impact that ideas associated with new museology, which moved into the mainstream in the 1990s, may have had on the architectural design and development of rhetoric employed by Quai Branly, Clifford proposed that 'the possibility of using the [architectural] boxes to create alternative, even critical or reflexive spaces holds potential for a less-totalizing museography' (Clifford 2007: 14).

Despite the indications of ongoing transformation in museum practice and scholarship, and also despite museum studies' relatively recent origins, its inherent and acknowledged interdisciplinarity, and the tendency of scholars to fetishize the contact zone concept proposed by Pratt (1991, 1992) and popularized by Clifford, museum studies has not found itself discussed in terms of its potential to function as a boundary discipline (noted also by

Whitehead 2007: 55). Reticence to adopt the boundary zone as a site of writing occurs also despite the interest expressed by writers from other disciplines keen to probe the intersections and allegiances between their own 'core' practices and the more marginal museum studies to appropriate (and in some cases challenge) its techniques. And although evidence of the trafficking of ideas between disciplines is widespread, museum studies is generally positioned as a relational rather than primary referent. For example, in a review article called 'Anthropology and the New Museology', Susan Applegate Krouse (2006: 170) asks, 'Is the new museology a theoretical orientation or a methodological orientation? . . . Whether we focus on theory or methodology, the new museology represents a particularly anthropological approach to museum work'. In another review article, 'Museology as Cultural Studies', anthropologist Eric Gable suggests that museum studies aligns most closely with cultural studies in that the goal of cultural studies is 'not only to bring into conscious awareness the extent of misrepresentation that occurs, but also to create representational space for silenced voices to be heard' (Gable 2009: 51). The observation appears to hide slight disappointment on the part of the reviewer, who approached the text with a single question in mind: '[D]oes anthropology still have anything to contribute to this burgeoning field?' (Gable 2009: 51). Identifying museum studies as a subcategory of cultural studies, Simon During asserts: 'In many of the most exciting research areas of the last few years – the study of museums is a good example – historians, literary critics, anthropologists, and geographers collaborate and compete with minimal disciplinary or methodological differences apparent' (During 1993: 25). The historian's perspective is provided by Randolph Starn who more cautiously claims: 'Museums and history are close kin, each with proprietary claims on gathering and interpreting materials from the past. By assembling objects outside everyday time and space, all museums are in some sense historical' (Starn 2005: n.p.).

This academic context leads to questions about the ways that contemporary museum studies represents its engagement with other disciplines. How does the discipline of museum studies negotiate the widespread interest in its subject matter and the methods and techniques it uses to investigate and convey meaning? How does it understand and address its status as an interdisciplinary field of research, as a boundary discipline? Although *Museum Revolutions* does not use the boundary discipline terminology that I advocate, the diversity (and, if we follow Rabinow 2007, adjacency) of its contents means that it occupies various border zones spanning present and past, theory and practice, culture and society. It is also the case that the contributors demonstrate various attempts to model the exchanges and transactions that occur between different kinds of institutions, as well as among institutions, publics, and communities. In so doing they actually demonstrate that museums are exemplary sites for interdisciplinary dialogues that both draw from and contribute to a number of fields, as well as to the frameworks and debates that characterize museum studies itself – notably between discursive or text-based and empirical or materialist approaches. In many cases, the essays within the text expertly occupy and investigate these sites, their contested meanings, and the mythologies that have often worked to isolate the experience of marginalized peoples.

Redefining categories

Although I am not sure that he would have used the same terminology I have employed in this book, Dening's approach (1998, 2000) to affective writing was a disruptive one that aimed to contribute to large-scale disciplinary/ discursive, institutional, and epistemological change by effecting a series of disobedient actions and expressions. He knew that change meant drawing into conversation the 'mythologizers' and current-day power brokers as much as it required returning a voice of sorts to 'the dead'. His project was a deeply ethical form of engaged research defined as a 'mechanism for a form of repetitive "troublemaking" that can activate theory and empirical data and open up the possibilities for meaningful social change' (Third 2016: 97). A boundary-crossing thinker and activist, Dening's work was 'tactical' in that it borrowed the spaces of the other (mainstream governmental order) to use or reuse them against that same order, to momentarily subvert it by bringing its assumptions into question:

> I make no secret that I want to change the world in my history-writing. In small ways – make it laugh, make it cry, make it serious for a moment, stop the dumbing down, spoil the mythologizers' day. But in bigger ways, too. I can't give life to the dead, but I can give them a voice. I can't give justice to the victims, but I can shake the living out of their moral lethargy to change the things in the present that are the consequences of the past.
>
> (Dening 2000: 216)

This passage demonstrates the role that affective writing has in processes of writing about experience, and, in so doing, it encourages discussion and about the contribution that the theme of borderwork might make to the activity of writing about museums. It reminds us of the scope and potential of processes of reflexive change and of the impact these approaches on Dening's own discipline of history, as well as on his individual research activity. Reading his work still reminds me that rather than being a single assault defined by loyalty to one 'side' or another (thereby completely unable to contemplate the prospect of working 'on' the border), revolutions occur in many registers, that they can be large or small, collective or individual, and that they can have different objects and exchanges in their line of sight. They are the precondition for a contemporary context in perpetual crisis. Moreover, these kinds of small disruptions – which are more tactical (disruptive) than strategic (structural) – influence the way we think, explain, and write about things as much as they alter the terms and conditions of collective experience itself.

Before I move to conclude this chapter, I want to think about the relationship between the small-scale affective political action (writing as action, everyday movement as action) of Dening and de Certeau and the contemporary context 'in perpetual crisis' that plays host to and motivates such activities.[13] This includes consideration of the place that museums, governmental institutions, and museum-like spaces play as boundary sites or border zones.[14] This requires attention also be paid to structural conditions of authority, knowledge, power, and definition (all are categories). While Dening's work (2000) provides an example of tactical or affective critique, a structural engagement with the question is provided by Claire Bishop's book, *Radical Museology*. Although both Dening and Bishop are motivated by what Bishop (2013: 23) calls the 'desire to understand our present condition and how to change it', she has described her project in more overtly political terms than those used by Dening (2000). Her book is 'a vivid manifesto for the contemporary as a *method* rather than a periodization, and for the importance of a politicized representation of history in museums of contemporary art' (my italics) (Bishop 2013: back cover blurb). Closer in genealogy to Foster's art theory and criticism than Dening's historical anthropology, Bishop's focus is on analyzing the definitions and uses of the term 'contemporary' in art museums today.

Rethinking the category of the contemporary (Bishop 2013), as well as the experience of it (Dening 2000), requires rearticulating Bishop's question about the role and place of institutions within the dialogue to ask where writing about museums sits and what it contributes. It means reflecting upon the ways that we engage critically, as writers and thinkers with our object of analysis, and examining what are the most appropriate political and social frame, disciplinary lens, and language for our task. In this book, our 'object' is not restricted to the contemporary art museums of Bishop's book but is concerned with the much broader category of museums in a contemporary context (including, for example, symbolic spaces like the Lincoln Memorial and attempts at creating new meaning for such spaces, as discussed in Chapter 1, or as demonstrated by the January 20, 2017 rallies and marches held to protest the inauguration of President Donald Trump) that is itself increasingly 'museum-like'. Because my primary concern is with the ways that meaning is created through a process of exchange, I am interested in Bishop's definition of 'dialectical contemporary', which does not designate a style or period so much as an approach that emphasizes the idea that 'artists might help us glimpse the contours of a project for rethinking our world [which] is surely one of the reasons why contemporary art, despite its near total imbrication in the market, continues to rouse such passionate interest and concern.' (Bishop 2013: 23). While this engagement is frequently present in museum studies scholarship, it is rarely made explicit. However, Bishop's statement helps show that in calling for museums to be increasingly socially relevant and engaged, museum studies scholars are actually also effectively demanding museums participate in 'the task of rethinking the category of "the contemporary"' (Bishop 2013: 6) as well as the category of 'museum'.

While using contemporary 'as a method' for a disobedient *museum* would mean insisting that an awareness of politics and the politics of representation be included in exhibitions and activities, contemporary as a method for the disobedient museum project for *writers* means engaging with the contemporary political context and recognizing the unique capacity of museums to speak across disciplinary boundaries (Faubion 2016). It is unique because in so doing – operating at this border zone (where it is influenced also by discussion of the contemporary as a field of adjacency Guyer 2016; Rabinow 2007) – it is developing a practice of 'affective writing' (a prerequisite for activist writing) that overcomes the gap between theory and practice (and in so doing, works toward building what Hall calls 'a practice in its own right' (Hall 1990: 18)).[15] It brings together the structural (Bishop) and the affective (Dening 1998, 2000) with the experiential (Rabinow 2007) by experimenting with new and not so new ways of 'making do' (de Certeau 1984), of unsettling normalized patterns of understanding and meaning (as Beck did with his subversion of the political left's techniques).

Sly as a fox

The main premise of *The Disobedient Museum: Writing at the Edge* is that both museums and writing about museums have the potential to offer new ways of understanding contemporary life. It is inspired by De Certeau, whose work exemplifies his canny suggestion: 'Sly as a fox and twice as quick: there are countless ways of "making do"' (1984: 29). Museums can 'make do' – and more – by insisting on an awareness of politics and the politics of representation in their exhibitions and activities. Writing about museums can also 'make do' – and more – by addressing museum practice in the context of and in dialogue with the broader political context and specific political activities occurring outside the museological space. Bringing the practice of writing into closer dialogue with the practice of museum work is particularly important where writers assert an obligation for political engagement by museums. This approach demands, however, an understanding that writing does not exist in parallel to museum work – it should not just talk 'about' its subject – but recognition that it also exists within a shared space of production/reception and should have a similar engagement with contemporary politics and social context, as well as museum practice. Writing is not a benign activity, and it certainly can become a tactical asset for social justice activists. Understanding the importance of how to engage with the contemporary world is one factor that is required for this endeavor, as is a better understanding about the role of writing/ engagement as critique.

I have modeled this approach for writing about museums in this short book. Influenced by Bishop's project of redefining the museum (but without taking that outcome as my own goal), the first chapter addressed the broader political context and focused on understanding the governmental and nongovernmental/radical cultures of this political landscape. I presented an engagement with contemporary critical responses in the media (news), as well as different activist positions (Beck 2010a, 2010b), as part of this culture before moving in Chapter 2 to show how the concept of 'crisis', which has been broadly deployed in disciplinary (humanities) as well as in social/political contexts, functioned as a kind of motivation for change/action. I addressed this context not as a separate element or neutral shell for museum action but to make the point that text (museum) and context (political environment) are always already intertwined and connected. In this final chapter, I have argued that it is imperative that writers understand this interrelationship because it shows how actions in one arena can and do impact on one another. Attention to interrelationships between terms allows an articulation of the unique location and value of museums, which often sit at the boundary of politics and culture, governmentality and nongovernmentality/radical thought, modernity/postmodernity (or 'hypermodernity'), and theory and practice. The value of this border position is key in the ability of museums (and museum writing) to be politically affective – it not only sits at this boundary, but its actions here have direct and indirect implications for the zones on either side – including what has already occurred in the past as well as actions that are yet to be undertaken.

This final chapter has highlighted Dening's work in particular to illustrate different ways of engaging with and performing disobedience as an alternative to the oppositional logic employed by 'antimuseum' language and tropes. My aim in highlighting his work through an exercise of reflection about an earlier process of review writing was to model a reflective and critical approach to writing about museums that extends the influence of his work for future museum scholars. This approach is inherently suited to the disobedient museum project, which is a project based on dirty thinking, that aims to encourage critical, reflective, engaged writing about museums, and which encourages thinking about what this form of affective writing might look like (and, by association, what kinds of methodological approaches it might take). Located at the site of specific boundary zones (museum, text, street, or other sites of cultural production), it transcends distinctions between theory and practice, inside and outside, past and present, and politics and culture. Aiming to avoid replicating the conditions of a cruel optimism, it seeks not to do more of the same or to promise a false alternative (it cannot exist outside because there is no outside) but to provide a way of reconfiguring understandings about political activism from within governmental sites of culture – such as museums but also including museum-like spaces including performative public protests on the National Mall in Washington, D.C., and other nationally significant or symbolic sites. de Certeau's tactical writing is key for offering pathways in which this project can be undertaken. Finally, while I opened this chapter by exploring the kind of possibility that a familiar if undervalued model of review writing (as a form of both encounter and critique) might provide, the exercise cannot be a prescriptive one, and it needs to be understood that no single template will be suited for the task. Affective (activist if you want to call it that) writing emphasizes the 'sustained state of relation as well as the passage (and the duration of passage) of forces and intensities' (Seigworth and Gregg 2010: 1), and ultimately this book has intended to provide a call to arms rather than a manifesto, handbook, or artillery.

Notes

1 Review writing is just one form of critical writing. Although it is often an imperfect and maligned form of critical writing, I have elected to focus on it in this chapter for the pragmatic and strategic reason that it has the potential to play a part in attempts to reinvigorate a critically engaged approach to writing about museums. In addition to being a relatively low-ranked activity for the reasons already described, journal editors in museum studies can find it difficult to solicit high-quality reviews. Unrefereed reviews often fall into the trap of centralizing the writer's opinion or of being descriptive over analytical, and they can demonstrate a lack of criticality about the authority of the writer. And yet, as reviews (of exhibitions, museums, and books as well as other events, outcomes, and media forms) are common features of our journals, they contribute to representing the current state of thinking in our field. Although the scholarly articles published in these journals (alongside books and other forms of expression)

also contribute to this image, reviews arguably are – or could be – more suited to work that is responsive in terms of the description that Third presents (see opening quote of chapter) for engaged research. As reviews are both a central component of our journals and an important element of the 'apprenticeship' that graduate study offers many students, I would like museum studies to explore the possibilities that review writing might play as a worksite to test out different approaches and methodologies for a renewed process of reflective critical writing that has positive effects for more extended forms of writing and rigorous analysis in other forums and contexts.

2 Arguing (Bowman 2015: 117):

> *October* did not merely report and analyze then-recent cultural developments but rather actively contributed and constituted those developments through a dialogical relationship between critics and artists. . . . [M]uch of our contemporary sense of what compromises postmodernism for the visual arts is fundamentally rooted in the intellectual positions advanced by *October* during 1976–1981.

3 Pezzini (2015: 6) explains that 'there still exists an abiding and deep-seated tension between definitions of "art criticism" and "art history" as is evident by the prevalence of the recent term, "art writing"'. A similar dichotomy exists within museum studies, such that museum writing remains a process that has been defined sketchily in relation to traditional writing about museum history (which typically draws on forms of writing associated with other disciplinary models such as art history or history). It is partly this indeterminacy that makes writing about museums so suitable as a site for exploring new modes of critical engagement across disciplines and normalized modes of expression.

4 Part of the reason for extending the discussion to other disciplines is the attempt to consider how crisis and regeneration have been dealt with in other contexts (for example, crisis has historically had a positive impact on broader humanities disciplines such as English literature).

5 It requires being aware of the following (Hage 2016):

> Writing evidence: How does one write about the acquisition and accumulation of data? How does one write about the different modes of relating to the world as a researcher and what are their ramifications on what one produces as accounts of reality? . . . Writing analysis: How does one write one's research experience? . . . Writing Theory: How does one integrate theory in the process of writing? How to make theory speak to social and cultural realities and vice versa. What does critiquing means? How to think with a multiplicity of theories. How to develop one's own theories.

6 This is the kind of work that has been favored by museums and museum writing that promote social justice agendas and object-based research (Peers and Brown 2003; Thomas 2010) and by critical theory scholars who promote embedded research (Felski 2016).

7 Dening's passage demonstrates the argument made by Messer-Davidow, Shumway and Sylvan (1993b: 3) that:

> To borrow from Foucault, we could say that disciplinarity is the means by which ensembles of diverse parts are brought into particular types of knowledge relations with each other. . . . If disciplines are such by virtue of a historically contingent, adventitious coherence of dispersed elements,

then to study that coherence is necessarily to begin questioning portrayals of disciplines as seamless, progressive, or naturally 'about' certain topics. In studying disciplinarity, one defamiliarizes disciplines; one distances oneself from them and problematizes their very existence.

8 'ANTIUNIVERSITY NOW is a collaborative experiment to revisit and reimagine the 1968 Anti-University of London in an ongoing programme of free and inclusive self-organised radical learning events. ANTIUNIVERSITY NOW challenges academic and class hierarchy through an open invitation to teach and learn any subject, in any form, anywhere' (www.antiuniversity.org). The impression of opposition was also apparent in the *Disobedient Objects* exhibition (www.vam. ac.uk/content/exhibitions/disobedient-objects), produced and shown at the Victoria and Albert Museum (and then widely toured globally), which, despite presenting the full richness of the object's own stories, decontextualized these stories from the museum context in which they were shown. Questions about what the radicality of the objects might mean for the host museum were not asked.

9 https://networks.h-net.org/node/73374/announcements/110733/writing-activism-motivating-social-and-political-shifts-graduate. Indeed, this urgency is recognized also by the increasing university-level courses and graduate conferences offering tuition in writing as activism, such as the Writing as Activism: Motivating Social and Political Shifts – Graduate Conference, convened in May 2016 by Brooklyn College (the quote I have used comes from the call for papers issued for this conference). Other examples include the New Urban Life Across the Globe: Activism and Change in a World of Cities graduate summer school convened by the IARU network/University of Copenhagen in July 2017, which I had the pleasure of contributing to. (Also see Flood, Martin, and Dreher 2013.)

10 Although having said that, some academics argue that all academic work is by default activist because the role of an engaged academic and an engaged university is to promote social justice, fairness, and attempt to speak truth to power (Arvanitakis 2013).

11 Much more can be said about the idea of the contemporary, in relation to contemporary art but particularly in the context of contemporary approaches to curatorial work. See Smith (2009: 241–71) and Smith (2015), which focuses on contemporary curatorial practices and is relevant to my later comments about Claire Bishop's *Radical Museology* (2013), which is addressed by Smith (2015: 24) as being notable for its argument about 'the failure of contemporary art historical scholarship to match the innovative work of radical museums'.

12 There is a substantial literature around relational museums that is based in museum anthropology. Howard Morphy explains that while 'ethnographic museums used to be seen as "us" studying "them", a more productive approach is to view museums as trans-cultural artefacts composed of relations between the museum and its source communities'. One example was The Relational Museum project (2002–2006), which charted the history and nature of the relations composing the Pitt Rivers Museum through analyzing the history of its collections (www.prm.ox.ac.uk/RelationalMuseum.html).

13 De Certeau's explanation of walking conforms with intellectual activism focused on processes of borderwork. He says (de Certeau 1984: 101):

> The long poem of walking manipulates spatial organizations, no matter how panoptic they may be: it is neither foreign to them (it can take place only within them) nor in conformity with them (it does not receive its identity from them). It creates shadows and ambiguities within them. It inserts

its multitudinous references and citations into them (social models, cultural mores, personal factors). Within them it is like a peddler, carrying something surprising, transverse or attractive compared with the usual choice. These diverse aspects provide the basis of a rhetoric. They can even be said to define it.

14 This work builds on Clifford's ideas about contact zones, about which I have written elsewhere, specifically in Message (2010), an essay that compares Clifford's work with that of postmodern art critic, Rosalind Krauss, another *October* contributor (and cofounder and contributing editor). Krauss's essay, 'The Cultural Logic of the Late Capitalist Museum' (1990), and Clifford's (2007) review article, 'Quai Branly in Process', mark a period of transformation in the way museums were defined and understood.

15 Smith has echoed Foster's complaint that contemporary art has lost its critical edge, which I explored earlier in regard to comments by Bowman (2015) on *October*. Although Foster addresses contemporary more as an outcome/effect caused by social events, Smith says (2016: 391):

> The area of contemporary culture that one would expect to be unequivocally contemporary, and which constantly proclaims itself as such – the visual arts – turns out to be conflicted and confused about the nature of its contemporaneity. Sadly, none of these sets of tools amount to a kit, nor do the partialities within each add up to one.

Movements are born in the moments when abstract principles become concrete concerns[1]

Figure E.1 Person holding 'Hope Demands Action' banner at Reclaim the Dream march finish point, which was the Martin Luther King, Jr. Memorial construction site, West Potomac Park, Washington, D.C., August 28, 2010

Photograph by Kylie Message.

This book opened with discussion about a photograph of a person attending a Tea Party rally at the Lincoln Memorial in Washington, D.C. seven years ago. It is an image, albeit an understated one, that has a place in the visual iconography of global mass protest. I interpreted the image as a sign of ambivalence in a visual field that has, over the course of the last few months, become crowded with unambiguous calls for political change. Looked at in the context of the recent surge of large-scale rallies for justice, equality, and human rights, the peeling 'I can see November from my House too!' sticker contributes to the increasingly explicit spectacle of active citizenship that has become a constant companion for crisis in contemporary life in the United States today. Despite the 1960s conviction that 'democracy is in the streets' (Cobb 2017) (which continues to be evident in the contestation over rally locations for the movements addressed in Chapter 1), the events of recent months build on the localized practices of the Occupy movements in 2011–2012[2] and ongoing actions like the Dakota Access Pipeline resistance, as well as the global Black Lives Matter movement to show something different. Democracy might happen in the streets or even in our museums, but, as Thrasher (2016) argues, this is far from enough. A key message made by political movements today is that the practices of democracy playing out on the streets need also to be extended into and reflected by our public offices and government agencies.

In this context, the images presented by political posters and photos of mass mobilization or indeed of the National Museum of African American History and Culture's 'celebration of blackness' (Thrasher 2016) become more than a site of political contestation in a world where crisis is an ordinary part of life. Images become mobile vehicles for possible challenges to and transgression of boundaries that typically work to distinguish official and independent places, definitions, and understandings about acceptable action.[3] Even after rallies draw to a close, images continue to convey meaning through their material residue (sometimes referred to as the archaeology of protest) and visual record, both of which are collected by museums and archives. Ongoing media reporting and reprisals by politicians or government officials shows that the influence of visual messages continues to impact the spaces where the action was or should have been. They continue to exert an affect the next day and the day after that, even after people have returned to their 'normal' lives.

It has not been my aim in this book to consider the material culture of protest (which was a focus of Message 2014); however, it is important to note that the material residue of reform movements – typically ephemera including posters, stickers, buttons, T-shirts – continues to reject the separation of binary oppositions such as public/political and us/them by demonstrating instances whereby what Ann Cvetkovich (2007: 464) calls 'what counts as national or public trauma', as that which is 'more visible and catastrophic . . . newsworthy and sensational' comes together with what she calls the 'small dramas' that 'draw attention to how structural forms of violence are so frequently lived, how their invisibility or normalization is another part of their oppressiveness'. The key thing here is to recognize that protest is itself fundamentally an attempt to transgress boundaries, to insist on the perceived inequity and injustice inherent in structural conditions of exclusion, opposition, and dominance (power, knowledge, economy). Even though 'demonstrations and assemblies are often not enough to produce radical change', as Butler (2017) argues, 'they do alter our perceptions about who *the people* are, and they assert fundamental freedoms that belong to bodies in their plurality'. They witness, enact, and perform an activity of tactical disobedience often at 'public' – that is, inherently contested – sites. Gaining leeway into government offices requires attracting the support of the 'moral majority' where possible, and this often means using affective and compelling visual media approaches to get into the 'hearts and minds' of people who will engage with and ideally, from the perspective of the movement, reproduce its causes in their diverse everyday spaces.

While the scope of this short book has not allowed a full discussion of the wider context of political activism practices or examples/movements (such as Black Lives Matter and the Dakota Access Pipeline resistance, but also including examples of activism against museums),[4] civil disobedience has been a significant influence in the development of the disobedient museum model. A generic definition of disobedience is a refusal to obey certain laws or governmental demands for the purpose of influencing legislation or government policy, characterized by the employment of such nonviolent techniques as boycotting, picketing, and nonpayment of taxes. However, disobedient practices that draw from tactical processes of subversion (civil disobedience) are not easily dichotomized into obedience/rebellion because they are not looking for clear 'alternative sites' of resistance that reinscribe oppositions around order/anarchy. Rallies and demonstrations fit with this description because activists typically demand changes in forms of governance and public cultural forms of knowledge rather than advocating the overthrow of the entire system (although exceptions obviously exist). I have modeled the disobedient museum concept on a tactical model of disruption that, similar to protests and rallies, takes place within structural conditions of oppression, which it does instead of aiming to identify 'alternative' or oppositional sites (such as an 'antimuseum'). As such, the disobedient model suits museums that have had – despite or perhaps because of the assumptions around national museums and governmentality – historically complex (and shifting) relationships with systems and structures and agents of power and that similarly escape facile attempts to define or categorize them according to polarized models. While a statement of opposition or revolution can be thwarted, suppressed, recuperated, or refuted, disobedience is aligned with processes of critique, which rely on processes of exchange and engagement rather than on opposition. As Bady (2013) explains:

Critique is not only a *part* of governance – and vice versa – but both are unthinkable without the other. Critique is actually dependent on power; as power over power, it can only alter the terms through which power is exercised. Instead of 'how not to be governed like that' – which might be expressive of a desire for the absence of governance – critique describes 'how to be governed, BUT how not to be governed not like that'.

Recognizing that critique is most effective when it uses the language and disciplinary instruments of the dominant order to hold this same order accountable, this book's primary goal has been to make a discipline-based contribution to museum studies. Rather than relying on a representational model that 'simultaneously reproduces the isolation of aesthetic modernism and a deficit modeling of culture' (Dewdney, Dibosa and Walsh 2013: 245) through its reliance on an intellectual paradigm of rationality and freedom, my approach, focused on the limits, edges, and failures of disciplinary thinking, does not escape a dominant order but seeks new tools to alter its conditions and the ways in which we articulate and analyze these conditions from and in relation to the interdisciplinary perspectives represented by the field. Related to this fundamentally reflective process of disciplinary critique is the book's attempt to make a case for the contribution that culture and discourses about culture can make to discourses of political action and activism. These aims share a process of theorization that has grown out of the case studies addressed in *Museums and Social Activism: Engaged Protest* (Message 2014), a book that explored interactions between political culture and cultural politics in the United States from the late 1950s through to 2013 to challenge the artificial distinction between culture and politics. The research presented in that book has formed the foundation for this one, which exists as something like an afterword, as well as an attempt to theorize its findings for the purposes of broader disciplinary debate.

I was close to finishing writing *The Disobedient Museum: Writing at the Edge* the month that Donald Trump was inaugurated, an event that generated an eruption of immediate responses that included the J20 actions focused on cultural sites and institutions, along with other events including the nationwide women's marches held on and beyond the National Mall. A great deal of media and scholarly coverage followed the inauguration and its resistance (including Cobb's 2017 essay on the return of civil disobedience), and a particularly insightful series of commentaries by writers grappling with various approaches for analyzing 'the rise of Trumpism' was published by *Cultural Anthropology*. Aligned with my intention to make a contribution to scholarly activism and disciplinary thought around the themes of politics, culture, and activism by exploring discursive relationships between museum studies, the political context, and social thought, the editors for that volume explained that in taking 'Trumpism' seriously, their contributors:

> make startling connections between present and past inequities, even as they formulate novel insights about what makes this moment distinct. In these ways, the series offers a much-needed corrective to many conventional explanations of the contemporary. The result is an urgent call to think politics, people, and scholarly praxis anew: one that may help guide critical engagements with the present and orient wider commitments to come.
>
> (Bessire and Bond 2017)

There are two particularly useful points in this passage. The first is the argument about an engaged form of critical practice, and the second is the imperative to rethink our engagement with the contemporary public sphere to better 'explain' its conditions, constraints, and experiences. Both these points expand upon general theoretical trends that I have explored throughout this book, from work on cultural anthropologist Paul Rabinow's (2007) analysis of the contemporary by Jane Guyer (2016) and others (Faubion 2016), through to art theorist Hal Foster's characterization of the current day as 'bad', and up to and including interdisciplinary theorists such as Berlant (2011) and others – Dening (1998, 2000) – who explore how to write *about* affect. In a statement pertaining to her project of articulating a radical museology out of contemporary art practices, Bishop makes a comment that is shared by many other 'rethinkers' of the contemporary: 'Looking at this global panorama of contemporary art museums, what binds them all together is less a concern for a collection, a history, a position, or a mission than a sense that contemporaneity is being staged on the level of image: the new, the cool, the photogenic, the well designed, the economically successful' (Bishop 2013: 12). This comment was prescient, given that Trump's inauguration coincided with the 50-year anniversary of the publication of Guy Debord's *Society of the Spectacle* (1994 [1967]), as well as a suite of key political/cultural activisms associated with the Situationist International movement in Europe and the Civil Rights movement in the United States throughout that year and period (1968 was the year of the Poor People's Campaign, May 12–June 24, as well as the assassinations of Martin Luther King, Jr., on April 4 and Robert F. Kennedy on June 5).[5]

In *The Society of the Spectacle*, Debord (1994) defined the spectacle as 'a social relationship between people that is mediated by images' (advertising, television, film, and celebrity) that function to distract and pacify the masses. He argued that the relationship between images is of equal if not greater importance in determining meaning than what is put forward by the discrete texts (referred to by Bishop, for example, as the collection, history, position, or museum mission statement) themselves. His focus was not, however, on visuality per se but on the ways that the social relations built around and between 'images' constituted what political philosopher Charles Taylor would later describe as a social imaginary. Social imaginaries are a social existence or reality imagined by people to describe 'how they fit together with others, how things go on between themselves and their fellows, the expectations that are normally met, and the deeper normative notions and images that underlie these expectations' (Taylor 2004: 23). The spectacle has not just become manifest in newer, bigger, more expensive museums (pace Bishop, see also Prior 2003; Prior 2006) but has – like the personal anxieties and political crises it ostensibly aims to subdue – come to exist as both an ordinary and defining (exceptional) feature of our present public culture. The changed contemporary context – this altogether 'other day' (Gellner 1965: 67 in Guyer 2016: 374) – presents some different challenges to those being rallied against in the streets, lecture theaters, and elsewhere in the 1960s. Yet Debord's conception of the spectacle remains consistent with Taylor's (2004) account of the social imaginary and Berlant's (2011) argument that cruel optimism is a process that subjects actively engage in to improve their lot but in so doing actually reinscribe structural forms of class, race, and gender oppression.[6] This means that while there may be fewer clear distinctions today between what is authentic/real and what is artificial, divisions and exclusions around us/them and power structures continue to exist and exert force.

The importance of tactical subversion as described by de Certeau, or the Situationist's concept of *détournement* – a term variously translated as 'diversion', 'detour', 'reroute', and 'hijack'[7] – offer possible ways of negotiating contemporary structures of power and governance (regardless of whether they are labeled as 'later-modernity', 'postmodernity', 'hypermodernity', or even just 'contemporary'). As 'grass-roots' forms of embodied critique, these movements disrupt the fabric of the everyday by creating a personal or collective crisis that aims to draw attention to the spectacle and the role we play in maintaining it through our social contracts. While de Certeau offers the simple cognitive act of walking off path as a form of tactical subversion, the Situationists championed activities such as repurposing old film reels, subverting iconic images or slogans, or devising literature inspired by the works of other writers. The role of visuality – including the imagery produced by movement across or occupation of symbolic sites – in contemporary protests, rallies, and demonstrations can be understood as aligned with these processes of subversion. The approach taken by protest movements to counteract messages of support for an incoming president (for example) by saturating social media with individualized and bespoke messages is effectively an attempt to *occupy* and disrupt the ubiquity of the spectacle. There is a risk that, in seeking to occupy/appropriate the spectacle by using its own terms of influence (signs, slogans, images) and the instruments (media) it uses to distract and pacify the masses, the causes represented by protest movements will be recuperated back into the spectacle (to become a mechanism in a process of cruel optimism), but for most social reform movements this is a risk that is worth taking.

Museums are as much a part of this everyday fabric of spectacle as are the protests and politics that often play out on their front doorsteps (Beck's Restoring Honor rally at the Lincoln Memorial in 2010, for instance, or the 2017 Women's March on the National Mall).[8] Located between 'the people' and their government (Message 2014), museums contribute to the lived experience of a social imaginary that is produced out of the epistemes, practices, discourses, and institutions that reproduce dominant power structures and their resultant inequalities. At the same time, however, recent decades have seen an escalation of statements by museums asserting their commitment to social justice causes and renewed remits for inclusion of hidden and difficult histories, as well as all facets of contemporary national life, including political protest and reform movements.[9] The 'double-faced' nature of museums means that they can act in support of reform movements, or they can contribute to the recuperation of their actions into mainstream national narratives. These agendas are not mutually exclusive (*Curatorial Activism* presents a case study of this paradox), and museums are frequently accused of being either 'too political' or 'not political enough' – sometimes the same museum will be accused of both these extremes. For example, the National Museum of Australia and the National Museum of the American Indian were subject to this simultaneously 'too much' and 'not enough' criticism when they opened in the aftermath of the culture and history wars in Australia and United States, respectively (Message 2006, and see Message 2014 for further examples).

The engagement of reform movements with the contemporary spectacle and the engagement of museums with political protest demonstrates that the process of talking across different sectors (text and context) requires a fundamentally interdisciplinary approach. The approach I am advocating is a form of borderwork that refuses to obey normal procedural boundaries on the one hand but that, on the other hand, employs the tactics used by theorists or protestors who seek to have a discursive impact by speaking from, to, and across divisions. The disobedient museum project aims to provide a workspace for exploring interaction across divisions. A conceptual idea as well as a model and a call for action (it can be literal or metaphoric), it offers an analogy to the museum-like activities described elsewhere. The disobedient museum is located, as such, at boundary sites that have traditionally separated culture from politics, but, rather than being contained by the edges, it bleeds out onto both sides by using the language of affect that is common to each. In occupying and exceeding this in-between zone, the conceptual disobedient museum model has the potential to contribute to build dialogue across areas that have traditionally had little discursive exchange (such as social movement studies and cultural studies, see Message 2015). Its relationship-building work emphasizes the connections between images/actions and analyzes how these links build the dominant social narratives (good life fantasies) that maintain and reproduce the conditions of the spectacle. The disobedient museum concept reveals the links between the macro (realm of governmentality) and micro (de Certeau's space of everyday transgression) in order to contribute to theoretical processes of critique that seek to explore the relationship between government/nongovernment actions and expressions of collective and individual identity in the contemporary world.

The imperative for intellectual activism that is apparent in *Cultural Anthropology*'s series on 'the rise of Trumpism', as well as the other work previously cited shows that the processes of critical thinking and analysis are as important for political activism today as they were 50 years ago. This work relates to the key questions of this book, which seeks to understand how a process of engaged critique might benefit museum studies and how museum studies might make a contribution to discourses of social and political change.[10] While I have looked elsewhere at the relationship between museums and politics (indeed this will continue to form the basis of my forthcoming case study-based work), this question about the role that museum studies plays in social critique and disciplinary relevance has been sitting increasingly uneasily in my mind for many years. A question of political urgency and methodological necessity, it has occupied my thoughts with an unease similar to that which I experienced in response to the 'I can see November from my House too!' image. Both experiences refute attempts to be categorized as exclusively cultural or political, and, as such, they embody moments of disruption to normative good life narratives and social discourses. These experiences have influenced the approach I have taken to writing this book, which is an attempt to experiment with a process of writing that seeks to produce an equivalent disruption to normative disciplinary models of attributing value and meaning.[11] Perhaps more importantly, *The Disobedient Museum: Writing at the Edge* is also an attempt to progress a political agenda of justice, equity, and human rights by exploring the role that culture and the processes of theoretical critique can have on political change. In the final instance, my approach has been to focus on the process of writing as a form of activism that brings together and elaborates on cultural and political agendas for change in order to offer an example of what can happen when abstract principles become concrete concerns.

Notes

1 Cobb (2017).
2 Occupy was a global movement that was manifested locally, the Dakota pipeline resistance was the opposite – a local cause that was manifested (gained support) globally.
3 See Message (2014: 46), which focused explicitly on behind-the-scenes interactions among museums, government institutions, and protest, where I argued that museums provided and advocated for a space of dialogue between culture and politics, between 'the people' and 'their government'.
4 It has not been my purpose in this short book to highlight specific causes or case studies, which is the approach taken in my subsequent titles. Another topic that is in need of further critical attention is the subject of protests that take place over and are aimed at museums. See existing work by Cooper (2008) and Lehrer (2015).
5 Vice President Joe Biden made a similar observation on December 6, 2016, less than a month after the presidential election. In New York to receive the Robert F. Kennedy Ripple of Hope Award, Biden said: 'I remind people, '68 was really a bad year. Really a bad year. And America didn't break. America didn't break' (Westcott 2016).
6 This process is also consistent with Benedict Anderson's representation of the nation as an 'imagined community' (1983).
7 The concept was initially devised by the Letterist International (founded by Debord) and later revised by the Situationists. In a 1957 essay entitled 'A User's Guide to Détournement', Debord and the artist Gil J. Wolman defined the concept as '[t]he mutual interference of two worlds of feeling, or the juxtaposition of two independent expressions, supersed[ing] the original elements and produc[ing] a synthetic organization of greater efficacy' (Debord and Wolman 1956).
8 For discussion about museums, the *Society of the Spectacle*, and the new museology, see Message (2006).
9 Evident, for example, in most Smithsonian Institution museums, including the National Museum of African American History and Culture (https://nmaahc.si.edu/about/museum), the National Museum of the American Indian (http://nmai.si.edu/about/mission/), and the Division of Political History at the National Museum of American History (http://americanhistory.si.edu/about/departments/political-history). For further discussion about mission statements and institutional remits, see Message (2014). This shift is also evident beyond the Smithsonian, in examples that include the Museum Social Action Project and The Museum of Impact (www.museumofimpact.org), as discussed by Murawski (2016a, 2016b).
10 While my purpose in this book has been to make a case for politically engaged writing about museums, rather than offer a template or how-to guide on writing this genre, I have attempted to articulate the approach that I used in *Museums and Social Activism: Engaged Protest* and that is also used in *Museums and Racism* and *Curatorial Activism* (both forthcoming 2018). These books model what this approach to engaged critical analysis 'looks like' in the context of the case studies that are addressed in each.
11 Here I have been influenced by Berlant (2012), who says:

> I hope my storytelling is good enough that you can imagine the *scene* or situation that compels thought. . . . I aim for the scene I'm describing to open up a question for you. If the questions become more vital and interesting in the reading, then I've done my job. If readers then encounter these questions in the world, they might have a different way to think and act in relation to them.

Bibliography

Adams, Geraldine Kendall (2016) 'Q&A with Dean Phelus', *Museums Association Blog*, December 7. Online at www.museumsassociation.org/museums-journal/q-a/07122016-q-and-a-dean-phelus-trump-presidency. Accessed February 21, 2017.

Ahmed, Sara (2010) *The Promise of Happiness*, Durham and London: Duke University Press.

Anderson, Benedict (1983) *Imagined Communities: Reflections on the Origin and Spread of Nationalism*, London and New York: Verso.

Anderson, Kurt (2011) 'The Protester', *Time*, December 14.

Ang, Ien (2006) 'From Cultural Studies to Cultural Research', *Cultural Studies Review*, vol. 12, no. 2: 183–97.

Apostolova, Vyara, Uberoi, Elise and Johnston, Neil (2017) 'Political Disengagement in the UK: Who Is Disengaged?', *House of Commons Library Briefing Paper, no. CBP7501*, April 26, London: UK Parliament. Online at http://researchbriefings.parliament.uk/ResearchBriefing/Summary/CBP-7501. Accessed May 12, 2017.

Appadurai, Arjun and Breckenridge, Carol (1992) 'Museums Are Good to Think: Heritage on View in India', in Ivan Karp, Christine Mullen Kreamer, and Steven D. Lavine (eds.) *Museums and Communities: The Politics of Public Culture*, Washington, DC, and London: Smithsonian Institution Press, pp. 34–55.

Arvanitakis, James (2013) 'Beyond Engagement: Universities Within Their Community', September 15. Online at http://jamesarvanitakis.net/beyond-engagement-universities-within-their-community/. Accessed February 21, 2017.

Bady, Aaron (2013) 'Bartleby in the University of California: The Social Life of Disobedience', *New Inquiry*, May 3. Online at https://thenewinquiry.com/blogs/zunguzungu/bartleby-in-the-university-of-california-the-social-life-of-disobedience/. Accessed February 21, 2017.

Barrett, Jennifer (2011a) *Museums and the Public Sphere*, Chichester, UK: John Wiley & Sons Ltd.

Barrett, Jennifer (2011b) ' "Protecting the Past, Safeguarding the Future": Museum Studies, the Profession and Museum Practice in Australia', in Des Griffin and Leon Paroissien (eds.) *Understanding Museums: Australian Museums and Museology*, Canberra, Australia: National Museum of Australia. Online at http://nma.gov.au/research/understanding-museums/JBarrett_2011.html. Accessed February 21, 2017.

Beck, Glenn (2010a) 'The Glenn Beck Program (Audio of Program from May 24)'. Online at http://mediamatters.org/mmtv/201005240029. Accessed February 21, 2017.

Beck, Glenn (2010b) 'The Glenn Beck Program (Audio of Program from May 26)'. Online at http://mediamatters.org/mmtv/201005260024. Accessed February 21, 2017.

Beck, Glenn (2010c) 'Glenn Beck Show on Fox News (video of program from August 30)'. Online at The Right Scoop, www.therightscoop.com/glenn-beck-the-smithsonian-called-about-828/. Accessed February 21, 2017.

Beck, Glenn (2010d) 'Keynote Address at the Restoring Honor to America Rally Delivered 28 August 2010', Lincoln Memorial, Washington, DC. Transcript. Online at www.americanrhetoric.com/speeches/glennbeckrestoringhonorkeynote. htm. Accessed February 21, 2017.

Belfiore, Eleonora and Bennett, Oliver (2008) *The Social Impact of the Arts: An Intellectual History*, Basingstoke, Hampshire: Palgrave Macmillan.

Belfiore, Eleonora and Upchurch, Anna (2013) *Humanities in the Twenty-First Century: Beyond Utility and Markets*, Basingstoke, Hampshire: Palgrave Macmillan.

Benjamin, Walter (1997) 'A Small History of Photography', in *One-Way Street and Other Writings*, trans. by E. Jephcott and K. Shorter, London and New York: Verso, pp. 24–57.

Bennett, Tony (1995) *The Birth of the Museum: History, Theory, Politics*, London and New York: Routledge.

Bennett, Tony (2005) 'Civic Laboratories: Museums, Cultural Objecthood and the Governance of the Social', *Cultural Studies*, vol. 19, no. 5: 521–47.

Bennett, Tony (2014) 'Liberal Government and the Practical History of Anthropology', *History and Anthropology*, vol. 25, no. 2: 150–70.

Bennett, Tony (2015a) 'Thinking (with) Museums: From Exhibitionary Complex to Governmental Assemblage', in A. Witcomb and K. Message (eds.) *Museum Theory*, Chichester, UK: John Wiley & Sons Ltd, pp. 3–20.

Bennett, Tony (2015b) 'Cultural Studies and the Culture Concept', *Cultural Studies*, vol. 29, no. 4: 546–68.

Bennett, Tony, Cameron, Fiona, Dias, Nelia, Dibley, Ben Dibley, Harrison, Rodney, Jacknis, Ira and McCarthy, Conal (2017) *Collecting, Ordering, Governing: Anthropology, Museums, and Liberal Government*, Durham: Duke University Press.

Bennett, Tony, Dibley, Ben and Harrison, Rodney (2014) 'Introduction: Anthropology, Collecting and Colonial Governmentalities', *History and Anthropology*, vol. 25, no. 2: 137–49.

Berlant, Lauren (n.d.) 'About', *Supervalent Thought Blog*. Online at https://supervalentthought.com/about/. Accessed February 21, 2017.

Berlant, Lauren (2006) 'Optimism and Its Objects', *Differences: A Journal of Feminist Cultural Studies*, vol. 17, no. 3: 20–36.

Berlant, Lauren (2007) 'On the Case', *Critical Inquiry*, vol. 33 (Summer): 663–72.

Berlant, Lauren (2008) 'Political Happiness – Or Cruel Optimism?', *Supervalent Thought Blog*, November 9. Online at https://supervalentthought.com/2008/11/09/political-happiness-or-cruel-optimism/. Accessed February 21, 2017.

Berlant, Lauren (2011) *Cruel Optimism*, Durham and London: Duke University Press.

Berlant, Lauren (2012) 'Lauren Berlant on Her Book *Cruel Optimism*', *Rorotoko*, June 5. Online at http://rorotoko.com/interview/20120605_berlant_lauren_on_cruel_optimism/. Accessed February 21, 2017.

Berlant, Lauren (2016) 'Trump, or Political Emotions', *Supervalent Thought Blog*, August 4. Online at https://supervalentthought.com/2016/08/04/trump-or-political-emotions/#more-964. Accessed February 21, 2017.

Berlant, Lauren and Greenwald, Jordan (2012) 'Affect in the End Times: A Conversation with Lauren Berlant', *Qui Parle: Critical Humanities and Social Sciences*, vol. 20, no. 2: 71–89.

Bessire, Lucas and Bond, David (eds.) (2017) 'The Rise of Trumpism', Hot Spots, *Cultural Anthropology* website, January 18. Online at https://culanth.org/fieldsights/1030-the-rise-of-trumpism. Accessed February 21, 2017.

Best, Steven and Kellner, Douglas (1991) 'Foucault and the Critique of Modernity' (ch. 2), in Steven Best and Douglas Kellner (eds.) *Postmodern Theory: Critical Interrogations*, London: Macmillan; New York: Guilford Press. Online at https://pages.gseis.ucla.edu/faculty/kellner/pomo/ch2.html. Accessed February 21, 2017.

Bevington, Douglas and Dixon, Chris (2007) 'Social Movement Studies: Rethinking Social Movement Scholarship and Activism', *Social Movement Studies: Journal of Social, Cultural and Political Protest*, vol. 4, no. 3: 185–208.

Bishop, Claire (2013) *Radical Museology: Or What's 'Contemporary' in Museums of Modern Art?* London: Koenig Books.

Boast, Robin (2011) 'Neocolonial Collaboration: Museum as Contact Zone Revisited', *Museum Anthropology*, vol. 34, no. 1: 56–70.

Boellstorff, Tom (2016) 'Isochronism as Analytic: Reflections on Rabinow's Contemporary', *HAU: Journal of Ethnographic Theory*, vol. 6, no. 1: 377–81.

Bourdieu, P. and Wacquant, L.J.D. (1992) *An Invitation to Reflexive Sociology*, Chicago: University of Chicago Press.

Bowman, Matthew (2015) 'October's Postmodernism', Visual Resources: An International Journal of Documentation, vol. 31, nos. 1–2: 117–26.

Butler, Judith (1993) Bodies That Matter: On the Discursive Limits of 'Sex', New York: Routledge.

Butler, Judith (2017) 'Reflections on Trump', Hot Spots, *Cultural Anthropology* website, January 18. Online at https://culanth.org/fieldsights/1032-reflections-on-trump. Accessed February 21, 2017.

Cameron, Fiona and McCarthy, Conal (2015) 'Introduction: New Research on Museums, Anthropology and Governmentality', *Museum & Society*, vol. 13, no. 1: 1–6.

Carlton, Alexandra (2016) '2016 May Have Been the Worst Year Yet, But Will It Get Better?', *news.com.au*, December 31. Online at www.news.com.au/lifestyle/real-life/news-life/2016-may-have-been-the-worst-year-yet-but-will-it-get-better/news-story/23c3a064aa535b22e2f18440beccc3e6/. Accessed February 21, 2017.

Carnegie Museum of Art (2017) 'What Is Authority? Speaking from the Museum', Seminar, *Carnegie Museum of Art*, February 9. Online at http://cmoa.org/event/what-is-authority-speaking-from-the-museum/. Accessed February 21, 2017.

Center for Information and Research on Civic Learning and Engagement (2016) '2016 Election. 2016 Millennial Poll Analysis: An In-Depth Look at Youth Attitudes, Tendencies, and Ideology', *The Center for Information and Research on Civic Learning and Engagement*, Jonathan M. Tisch College of Civic Life, Medford, Massachusetts: Tufts University. Online at http://civicyouth.org/wp-content/uploads/2016/10/2016-Millennial-Poll-Analysis.pdf. Accessed May 12, 2017.

Clifford, James (1988) *The Predicament of Culture: Twentieth-Century Ethnography, Literature and Art*, Cambridge, MA: Harvard University Press.

Clifford, James (1997) *Routes: Travel and Translation in the Late Twentieth Century*, Cambridge, MA: Harvard University Press.

Clifford, James (2004) 'Looking Several Ways: Anthropology and Native Heritage in Alaska', *Current Anthropology*, vol. 45, no. 1: 5–23, 26–8.

Clifford, James (2007) 'Quai Branly in Process', *October*, vol. 120 (Spring): 3–23.

Cobb, Jelani (2017) 'The Return of Civil Disobedience', *New Yorker*, January 9. Online at www.newyorker.com/magazine/2017/01/09/the-return-of-civil-disobedience. Accessed February 21, 2017.

Cooper, Karen C. (2008) *Spirited Encounters: American Indians Protest Museum Policies and Practices*, Lanham, MD: AltaMira.

Cunningham, Vinson (2016) 'Making a Home for Black History: The Vision and the Challenges Behind a New Museum on the National Mall', *New Yorker*, August 29. Online at www.newyorker.com/magazine/2016/08/29/analyzing-the-national-museum-of-african-american-history-and-culture. Accessed February 21, 2017.

Cvetkovich, Ann (2007) 'Public Feelings', *South Atlantic Quarterly*, vol. 106, no. 3: 459–68.

Davis, Ben (2016a) 'This Is the Art That Mattered From the 2016 Presidential Election', *Artnet News*, November 7. Online at https://news.artnet.com/art-world/election-art-2016-734828. Accessed February 21, 2017.

Davis, Ben (2016b) 'Art Must Admit the Lesson of Donald Trump's Election or Face Irrelevance', *Artnet News*, November 29. Online at https://news.artnet.com/art-world/art-must-admit-trump-lesson-764063. Accessed February 21, 2017.

Davis, Ben (2017) 'Richard Serra, Cindy Sherman, and Dozens of Others Call for Action on Inauguration Day', *Artnet News*, January 6. Online at https://news.artnet.com/art-world/call-for-action-inauguration-day-808625. Accessed February 21, 2017.

Debord, Guy (1994 [1967]) *The Society of the Spectacle*, trans. by D. Nicholson-Smith, New York: Zone Books.

Debord, Guy and Wolman, Gil J. (1956) 'A User's Guide to Détournement', *Bureau of Public Secrets*, n.d. Online at www.bopsecrets.org/cat.htm. Accessed February 21, 2017.

de Certeau, Michel (1984) *The Practice of Everyday Life*, trans. by S. Rendall, Berkeley and Los Angeles: University of California Press.

Deliss, Clémentine and Keck, Frédéric (2016) 'Remediation, and Some Problems Post-Ethnographic Museums Face', *Hau: Journal of Ethnographic Theory*, vol. 6, no. 1: 387–90.

Dening, Greg (1996) *Performances*, Carlton, Victoria: Melbourne University Press.

Dening, Greg (1998) 'Writing, Rewriting the Beach', *Rethinking History*, vol. 2, no. 2: 143–72.

Dening, Greg (2000) 'Review: Enigma Variations on History in Three Keys: A Conversational Essay', *History and Theory*, vol. 39, no. 2: 210–17.

Dening, Greg (2004) *Beach Crossings: Voyaging Across Times, Cultures, and Self*, Philadelphia: University of Pennsylvania Press.

Desvallées, André and Mairesse, François (2009) *Key Concepts of Museology*, trans. by S. Nash, Paris: Armand Colin and ICOM.

Dewdney, Andrew, Dibosa, David, and Walsh, Victoria (2013) *Post Critical Museology: Theory and Practice in the Art Museum*, London and New York: Routledge.

During, Simon (1993) 'Introduction', in Simon During (ed.) *The Cultural Studies Reader*, London and New York: Routledge, pp. 1–28.

During, Simon (2006) 'Is Cultural Studies a Discipline?: And Does It Make Any Political Difference?', *Cultural Politics*, vol. 2, no. 3: 265–80.

Executive Office of the President (2017) 'Executive Order 13769 of January 27, 2017. Protecting the Nation from Foreign Terrorist Entry into the United States', *Federal Register*, vol. 82, no. 20, February 1. Online at www.gpo.gov/fdsys/pkg/FR-2017-02-01/pdf/2017-02281.pdf. Accessed February 21, 2017.

Faubion, James D. (2016) 'Introduction: On the Anthropology of the Contemporary: Addressing Concepts, Designs, and Practices', *Hau: Journal of Ethnographic Theory*, vol. 6, no. 1: 371–3.

Felski, Rita (2016) *The Limits of Critique*, Chicago: University of Chicago Press.

Fielding, Steven (2007) 'Review Article: Looking for the "New Political History"', *Journal of Contemporary History*, vol. 42, no. 3: 515–24.

Flood, Michael, Martin, Brian and Dreher, Tanja (2013) 'Combining Academia and Activism: Common Obstacles and Useful Tools', *Australian Universities' Review*, vol. 55, no. 1: 17–26.

Foster, Hal (2015) *Bad New Days: Art, Criticism, Emergency*, London and New York: Verso.

Foucault, Michel (1977) 'Nietzsche, Genealogy, History', in D.F. Bouchard (ed.) *Language, Counter-Memory, Practice: Selected Essays and Interviews*, Ithaca, NY: Cornell University Press, pp. 139–64.

Fraser, Andrea (2005) 'From the Critique of Institutions to an Institution of Critique', *Artforum*, vol. 44, no. 1.

Fraser, Pamela and Rothman, Roger (2017) 'Introduction: Beyond Critique', in P. Fraser and R. Rothman (eds.) *Beyond Critique: Contemporary Art in Theory, Practice, and Instruction*, New York and London: Bloomsbury Academic, pp. 1–12.

Fyfe, Gordon (1996), 'A Trojan Horse at the Tate: theorizing the museum as agency and structure', in Sharon Macdonald and Gordon Fyfe (eds.) Representing Identity and Diversity in a Changing World, Oxford: Blackwell Sociological Review, pp. 203–228.

Gable, Eric (2009) 'Review Essay: Museology as Cultural Studies', *Museum Anthropology*, vol. 32, no. 1: 51–4.

Gellner, Ernest (1965) *Thought and Change*, Chicago: University of Chicago Press.

Gentry, Kynan (2015) '"The Pathos of Conservation": Raphael Samuel and the Politics of Heritage', *International Journal of Heritage Studies*, vol. 21, no. 6: 561–76.

Glanton, Dahleen (2016) 'White Women, Own up to It: You're the Reason Hillary Clinton Lost', *Chicago Tribune*, November 18. Online at www.chicagotribune.

com/news/columnists/glanton/ct-white-women-glanton-20161118-column.html. Accessed February 21, 2017.

Gledhill, Jim (2012) 'Collecting Occupy London: Public Collecting Institutions and Social Protest Movements in the 21st Century', *Social Movement Studies*, vol. 11, nos. 3–4: 342–8.

Gonzalez, Umberto (2016) 'Amanda Palmer Ripped for Saying Trump Will "Make Punk Rock Great Again"', *The Wrap*, December 29. Online at www.thewrap. com/amanda-palmer-donald-trump/. Accessed February 21, 2017.

Gosden, C., Larson, F. with A. Petch (2007) *Knowing Things: Exploring the Collections at the Pitt Rivers Museum, 1884–1945*, Oxford: Oxford University Press.

Graeber, David (2008) *Possibilities: Essays on Hierarchy, Rebellion, and Desire*, Oakland, CA: AK Press.

Gray, Clive (2002) 'Local Government and the Arts', *Local Government Studies*, vol. 28, no. 1: 77–90.

Gray, Clive (2011) 'Museums, Galleries, Politics and Management', *Public Policy and Administration*, vol. 26, no. 1: 45–61.

Groer, Annie (2010) 'Smithsonian Snags Memorabilia from Glenn Beck, Al Sharpton Rallies', *Politics Daily*, August 31.

Grossberg, Lawrence (2006) 'Does Cultural Studies Have Futures? Should It? (or What's the Matter with New York?) Cultural Studies, Contexts and Conjunctures', *Cultural Studies*, vol. 20, no. 1: 1–32.

Gurian, Elaine Heumann (2006) *Civilizing the Museum: The Collected Writings of Elaine Heumann Gurian*, London: Routledge.

Guyer, Jane I. (2016) '"On the Verge": From the Possible to the Emergent', *Hau: Journal of Ethnographic Theory*, vol. 6, no. 1: 373–7.

Haacke, Hans (1983) 'All the Art That's Fit to Show', in A.A. Bronson and Peggy Gale (eds.) *Museums by Artists*, Toronto: Art Metropole, pp. 149–84.

Haenfler, R., Johnson, B. and Jones, E. (2012) 'Lifestyle Movements: Exploring the Intersection of Lifestyle and Social Movements', *Social Movement Studies*, vol. 11, no. 1: 1–20.

Hage, Ghasson (2016) 'Reflexive Writing', keynote presentation at the Crossroads in Cultural Studies Conference, Western Sydney University, December 13. Online at www.westernsydney.edu.au/ics/news_and_media/news/2017/ghassan_ hage_on_reflexive_writing. Accessed February 21, 2017.

Hall, Stuart (1990) 'The Emergence of Cultural Studies and the Crisis of the Humanities', *October*, vol. 53 (Summer): 11–23.

Hall, Stuart (1992) 'Cultural Studies and Its Theoretical Legacies', in Lawrence Grossberg, Cary Nelson, and Paula Treichler (eds.) *Cultural Studies*, New York and London: Routledge.

Halloran, Liz (2010) 'Glenn Beck Comes to DC, Controversy Follows', *NPR*, August 27.

Harmon, Steph (2016) 'Amanda Palmer: "Donald Trump Is Going to Make Punk Rock Great Again"', *Guardian*, December 29. Online at www.theguardian.com/ music/australia-news-blog/2016/dec/29/amanda-palmer-donald-trump-is-going-to-make-punk-rock-great-again?CMP=twt_gu. Accessed February 21, 2017.

Harrison, Faye V. (1993) 'Writing Against the Grain: Cultural Politics of Difference in the Work of Alice Walker', *Critique of Anthropology*, vol. 13, no. 4: 401–27.

Hayden, Tom (2011) 'Obama Between Movements and Machiavellians', *The South Atlantic Quarterly*, vol. 110, no. 1 (Winter): 265–71.

J20 Art Strike (2017a) 'J20 Art Strike: An Invitation to Cultural Institutions'. Online at https://j20artstrike.org. Accessed February 21, 2017.

J20 Art Strike (2017b) 'On J20 and Beyond: A Declaration of the Arts Against Trumpism'. Online at https://j20artstrike.org/J20_UNGOVERNABLE_ANTI-FASCIST.pdf. Accessed February 21, 2017.

Jeffries, Stuart (2015) 'David Graeber: "So Many People Spend Their Working Lives Doing Jobs They Think Are Unnecessary"', *Guardian*, March 21. Online at www.theguardian.com/books/2015/mar/21/books-interview-david-graeber-the-utopia-of-rules?paging=off. Accessed February 21, 2017.

Jennings, Gretchen (2015) 'The #museumsrespondtoFerguson Initiative, a Necessary Conversation', *Museums & Social Issues*, vol. 10, no. 2: 97–105.

Jõekalda, Kristina (2013) 'What Has Become of the New Art History?', *Journal of Art Historiography*, no. 9, December. Online at https://arthistoriography.files.wordpress.com/2013/12/jc3b5ekalda.pdf. Accessed February 21, 2017.

Judah, Hettie (2016) 'The 13 Most Overused Words in the Art World in 2016', *Artnet.news*. Online at https://news.artnet.com/art-world/13-words-the-art-world-overused-792455. Accessed February 21, 2017.

Judkis, M. (2011) 'Occupy Wall Street Signs: Which Should Go in the Smithsonian?', *Washington Post*, October 24.

Kahlenberg, Richard D. and Janey, Clifford (2016) 'Is Trump's Victory the Jump-Start Civics Education Needed?' *The Atlantic*, November 10. Online at www.theatlantic.com/education/archive/2016/11/is-trumps-victory-the-jump-start-civics-education-needed/507293/. Accessed May 12, 2017.

Knell, Simon J., MacLeod, Suzanne, and Watson, Sheila (eds.) (2007a) *Museum Revolutions: How Museums Change and Are Changed*, London and New York: Routledge.

Knell, Simon J., MacLeod, Suzanne, and Watson, Sheila (2007b) 'Introduction', in S.J. Knell, S. MacLeod, and S. Watson (eds.) *Museum Revolutions: How Museums Change and Are Changed*, London and New York: Routledge, pp. xix–xxvi.

Koselleck, Reinhart (1988 [1959]) *Critique and Crisis: Enlightenment and the Pathogenesis of Modern Society*, Cambridge MA: Berg Publishers.

Kratz, Corinne A. and Karp, Ivan (2006) 'Introduction: Museum Frictions: Public Cultures/Global Transformations', in I. Karp, C.A. Kratz, L. Szwaja, and T. Ybarra-Frausto (eds.) *Museum Frictions: Public Cultures/Global Transformations*, Durham and London: Duke University Press, pp. 1–34.

Krauss, Rosalind (1990) 'Cultural Logic of the Late Capitalist Museum', *October*, vol. 54 (Fall).

Krouse, Susan A. (2006) 'Anthropology and the New Museology', *Reviews in Anthropology*, vol. 35, no. 2: 169–82.

Lassiter, Matthew D. (2011) 'Who Speaks for the Silent Majority?', *New York Times*, November 2. Online at www.nytimes.com/2011/11/03/opinion/populism-and-the-silent-majority.html. Accessed February 21, 2017.

Lehrer, Erica (2015) 'Thinking Through the Canadian Museum for Human Rights', *American Quarterly*, vol. 67, no. 4: 195–216.

Ley, James (2016) 'Expert Textpert', *The Sydney Review of Books*, April 13. Online at http://sydneyreviewofbooks.com/the-limits-of-critique-the-art-of-reading/. Accessed February 21, 2017.

Linenthal, Edward (1995) *Preserving Memory: The Struggle to Create America's Holocaust Museum*, New York: Columbia University Press.

Lonetree, Amy and Cobb, Amanda J. (eds.) (2008) *The National Museum of the American Indian: Critical Conversations*, Lincoln: University of Nebraska Press.

Lord, Beth (2007) 'From the Document to the Monument: Museums and the Philosophy of History', in S.J. Knell, S. MacLeod, and S. Watson (eds.) *Museum Revolutions: How Museums Change and Are Changed*, London and New York: Routledge, pp. 355–66.

Luhmann, Niklas (1990) *Essays on Self-Reference*, New York: Columbia University Press.

Luke, Timothy W. (2002) *Museum Politics: Power Plays at the Exhibition*, Minneapolis: University of Minnesota Press.

MacAskill, Ewen (2010) 'US Right Claims Spirit of Martin Luther King at Lincoln Memorial Rally', *Guardian*, August 28.

Macdonald, Sharon (ed.) (2006) *A Companion to Museum Studies*, Oxford: Blackwell.

Macdonald, Sharon (2008) *Difficult Heritage: Negotiating the Nazi Past in Nuremberg and Beyond*, London and New York: Routledge.

Macintyre, Stuart and Clark, Anna (2003) *The History Wars*, Carlton, Victoria: Melbourne University Press.

Mbembe, Achille and Roitman, Janet (1995) 'Figures of the Subject in Times of Crisis', *Public Culture*, vol. 7, no. 2 (Winter): 323–52.

McCarthy, Conal (2011) *Museums and Maori: Heritage Professionals, Indigenous Collections, Current Practice*, Wellington: Te Papa Press; Walnut Creek, CA: Left Coast Press.

McSherry, Corynne (2001) *Who Owns Academic Work? Battling for Control of Intellectual Property*, Cambridge, MA: Harvard University Press.

Message, Kylie (2006) *New Museums and the Making of Culture*, Oxford and New York: Berg.

Message, Kylie (2009a) 'Museum Studies: Borderwork, Genealogy, Revolution', *Museum and Society*, vol. 7, no. 2: 125–32.

Message, Kylie (2009b) 'Culture, Citizenship and Australian Multiculturalism: The Contest over Identity Formation at the National Museum of Australia', *Humanities Research*, vol. XV, no. 2: 23–48.

Message, Kylie (2010) 'Museums in the Twenty-First Century: Still Looking for Signs of Difference', *Konsthistorisk tidskrift – Journal of Art History*, vol. 78: 204–21.

Message, Kylie (2013) 'Slipping Through the Cracks: Museums and Social Inclusion in Australian Cultural Policy Development 2007–2010', *International Journal of Cultural Policy*, vol. 19, no. 2: 201–21.

Message, Kylie (2014) *Museums and Social Activism: Engaged Protest*, London and New York: Routledge.

Message, Kylie (2015) 'Contentious Politics and Museums as Contact Zones', in A. Witcomb and K. Message (eds.) *Museum Theory*, Chichester, UK: John Wiley & Sons Ltd, pp. 253–82.

Message, Kylie (forthcoming 2018a) *Museums and Racism*, London and New York: Routledge.

Message, Kylie (forthcoming 2018b) *Curatorial Activism*, London and New York: Routledge.

Message, Kylie and Witcomb, Andrea (2015) 'Introduction: Museum Theory: An Expanded Field', in A. Witcomb and K. Message (eds.) *Museum Theory*, Chichester, UK: John Wiley & Sons Ltd, pp. xxxv–xiii.

Messer-Davidow, Ellen, Shumway, David R., and Sylvan, David J. (eds.) (1993a) *Knowledges: Historical and Critical Studies in Disciplinarity*, Charlottesville, VA: University of Virginia Press.

Messer-Davidow, Ellen, Shumway, David R., and Sylvan, David J. (1993b) 'Introduction: Disciplinary Ways of Knowing', in E. Messer-Davidow, D.R. Shumway, and D.J. Sylvan (eds.) *Knowledges: Historical and Critical Studies in Disciplinarity*, Charlottesville, VA: University of Virginia Press, pp. 1–21.

Miah, Andy (2009) 'We're All Activists Now', *Guardian*, March 21, Online at www.theguardian.com/science/2009/mar/20/ethical-living-food-animal-welfare. Accessed February 21, 2017.

Milbank, Dana (2010) 'Civil Rights' New "Owner": Glenn Beck', *Washington Post*, August 29.

Mitchell, W.J.T. (1995) 'Interdisciplinarity and Visual Culture', *Art Bulletin*, vol. LXXVII, no. 4: 540–4.

Morphy, Howard (2015) 'The Displaced Local: Multiple Agency in the Building of Museums' Ethnographic Collections', in A. Witcomb and K. Message (eds.) *Museum Theory*, Chichester, UK: John Wiley & Sons Ltd, pp. 365–88.

Mullins, Matthew (2015) 'Are We Postcritical?', *Los Angeles Review of Books*, December 27. Online at https://lareviewofbooks.org/article/are-we-postcritical. Accessed February 21, 2017.

Murawska-Muthesius, Katarzyna and Piotrowski, Piotr (eds.) (2015) *From Museum Critique to the Critical Museum*, London and New York: Routledge.

Murawski, Mike (2016a) 'Museums Go to Work', *MuseumNext* Keynote address, Tribeca Center for Performing Arts, New York, NY, November 28. Online at https://artmuseumteaching.com/2016/11/28/this-is-the-time-when-museums-go-to-work-museumnext-keynote-address/. Accessed February 21, 2017.

Murawski, Mike (2016b) 'Urgency of Empathy and Social Action in Museums', Tribeca Center for Performing Arts, New York, NY, November 15. Online at https://artmuseumteaching.com/author/murawski27/. Accessed February 21, 2017.

MuseumNext (2017) 'Should Museums Be Activists?'. Online at www.museumnext. com/2017/04/should-museums-be-activists/. Accessed May 12, 2017.

Newman, Andrew and Selwood, Sara (eds.) (2008) 'The Consequences of Instrumental Museum and Gallery Policy', Special issue, *Cultural Trends*, vol. 17, no. 4.

Nixon, Richard (1969) 'Address to the Nation on the War in Vietnam', November 3. Online at http://watergate.info/1969/11/03/nixons-silent-majority-speech.html. Accessed February 21, 2017.

Obama, Barack (2004) 'Keynote Address at the Democratic National Convention (transcript "Illinois Senate Candidate Barack Obama")', Boston: FDCH E-Media. Online at www.washingtonpost.com/wp-dyn/articles/A19751-2004Jul27.html. Accessed February 21, 2017.

Obama, Barack (2007) 'Campaign Speech Transcript', *Guardian*, February 11. Online at www.theguardian.com/world/2007/feb/10/barackobama. Accessed February 21, 2017.

Onciul, Bryony (2015) *Museums, Heritage and Indigenous Voice Decolonizing Engagement*, London and New York: Routledge.

Peers, Laura and Brown, Alison K. (eds.) (2003) *Museums and Source Communities*, New York and London: Routledge.

Pezzini, Barbara (2015) 'Introduction, Visual Resources: An International Journal of Documentation', *Visual Resources: An International Journal of Documentation*, vol. 31, nos. 1–2: 3–13.

Pickerill, Jenny and Krinsky, John (2012) 'Why Does Occupy Matter?', *Social Movement Studies*, vol. 11, nos. 3–4: 279–87.

Political Concepts (2011) 'Editorial Statement', *Political Concepts: A Critical Lexicon*, vol. 1. Online at www.politicalconcepts.org/editorial-preface/. Accessed February 21, 2017.

Polletta, Francesca (1997) 'Culture and Its Discontents: Recent Theorizing on the Cultural Dimensions of Protest', *Sociological Inquiry*, vol. 67, no. 4: 431–50.

Post, Robert (2009) 'Debating Disciplinarity', *Critical Inquiry*, vol. 35, no. 4: 749–70.

Power, Nina (2011) 'The Meaning of *Time* Magazine's Celebration of the Protester', *Guardian*, December 17. Online at www.theguardian.com/comme'tisfree/2011/dec/16/meaning-time-magazine-celebration-protester. Accessed February 21, 2017.

Pratt, Mary Louise (1991) 'Arts of the Contact Zone', *Profession*, vol. 91: 33–40.

Pratt, Mary Louise (1992) *Imperial Eyes: Travel Writing and Transculturation*, London: Routledge.

Preziosi, Donald (2006) 'Art History and Museology: Rendering the Visible Legible', in S. Macdonald (ed.) *A Companion to Museum Studies*, Oxford: Blackwell, pp. 50–63.

Prior, Nick (2003) 'Having One's Tate and Eating It: Transformations of the Museum in the Hypermodern Era', in Andrew McClellan (ed.) *Art and Its Publics: Museum Studies at the End of the Millennium*, Oxford and Malden, MA: Blackwell, pp. 51–74.

Prior, Nick (2006) 'Postmodern Restructurings', in S. Macdonald (ed.) *A Companion to Museum Studies*, Oxford: Blackwell, pp. 509–24.

Rabinow, Paul (2007) *Marking Time: On the Anthropology of the Contemporary*, Princeton, NJ: Princeton University Press.

Rabinow, Paul (2012) 'A Contemporary Museum', in C. Deliss (ed.) *Object Atlas: Fieldwork in the Museum*, Bielefeld: Kerber, pp. 1–8.

Rappeport, Alan (2016) 'Who Won the Debate? Hillary Clinton, the "Nasty Woman" ', *New York Times*, October 20. Online at www.nytimes.com/2016/10/21/us/politics/who-won-the-third-debate.html. Accessed February 21, 2017.

Rees, A.L. and Borzello, F. (eds.) (1986) *The New Art History*, London: Camden Press.

Rich, Frank (2010) 'The Billionaires Bankrolling the Tea Party', *New York Times*, August 29.

Richardson, Michael (2015) 'Criticism Beyond Judgment: Reading, Writing and the Affective Turn', Seminar, Western Sydney University. Online at www.westernsydney.edu.au/writing_and_society/events/writing_and_society_seminars/2015_seminars/michael_richardson_on_reading,_writing_and_the_affective_turn. Accessed February 21, 2017.

Robbins, Bruce (2016) 'A Starting Point for Politics: The Radical Life and Times of Stuart Hall', *The Nation*, October 27. Online at www.thenation.com/article/the-radical-life-of-stuart-hall/. Accessed February 21, 2017.

Roitman, Janet (2012) 'Crisis', *Political Concepts: A Critical Lexicon*, vol. 1. Online at www.politicalconcepts.org/issue1/crisis/. Accessed February 21, 2017.

Samuel, Raphael (1994) *Theatres of Memory: Volume 1: Past and Present in Contemporary Culture*, London: Verso.

Sandell, Richard (2016) *Museums, Moralities and Human Rights*, London and New York: Routledge.

Sandell, Richard and Janes, Robert (eds.) (forthcoming 2018) *Museums and Activism*, London and New York: Routledge.

Sandell, Richard and Nightingale, Eithne (eds.) (2012) *Museums, Equality and Social Justice*, London and New York: Routledge.

Science Europe Scientific Committee for the Humanities (2015) 'Radical Innovation: Humanities Research Crossing Knowledge Boundaries and Fostering Deep Change', Science Europe – Scientific Committee for the Humanities, D/2015/13. 324/12. Online at www.scienceeurope.org/uploads/PublicDocumentsAndSpeeches/SCsPublicDocs/151222_HUMAN_OP_Radical_Innovation_web.pdf. Accessed February 21, 2017.

Seigworth, Gregory J. and Gregg, Melissa (2010) 'An Inventory of Shimmers', in Melissa Gregg and Gregory J. Seigworth (eds.) The Affect Theory Reader. Durham, North Carolina: Duke University Press, pp.1–28.

Selisker, Scott (2016) 'Notes on Felski's *The Limits of Critique*', January 24. Online at http://u.arizona.edu/~selisker/post/felskicritique/. Accessed February 21, 2017.

Smith, Terry (2009) *What Is Contemporary Art?* Chicago and London: The University of Chicago Press.

Smith, Terry (2015) *Talking Contemporary Curating*, ICI Perspectives in Curating no. 2, New York: Independent Curators International.

Smith, Terry (2016) 'Art, Anthropology, and Anxiety', *Hau: Journal of Ethnographic Theory*, vol. 6, no. 1: 390–8.

Snow, David A. (2004) 'Social Movements as Challenges to Authority: Resistance to an Emerging Conceptual Hegemony', *Research in Social Movements, Conflicts and Change*, vol. 25: 3–25.

Solnit, Rebecca (2006) *Hope in the Dark: Untold Histories, Wild Possibilities*, New York: Nation Books.

Solnit, Rebecca (2012) 'We Could Be Heroes: An Election-year Letter', *Guardian*, October 15. Online at www.theguardian.com/commentisfree/2012/oct/15/letter-dismal-allies-us-left. Accessed February 21, 2017.

Solnit, Rebecca (2016a) *Hope in the Dark: Untold Histories, Wild Possibilities* (new edition), Edinburgh and London: Canongate Books.

Solnit, Rebecca (2016b) '"Hope Is an Embrace of the Unknown": Rebecca Solnit on Living in Dark Times', *Guardian*, July 15. Online at www.theguardian.

com/books/2016/jul/15/rebecca-solnit-hope-in-the-dark-new-essay-embrace-unknown. Accessed February 21, 2017.

Sørensen, Marie Louise Stig and Carman, John (2009a) 'Setting the scene', in Marie Louise Stig Sørensen and John Carman (eds.) *Heritage Studies: Methods and Approaches*, London and New York: Routledge, pp. 1–2.

Sørensen, Marie Louise Stig and Carman, John (2009b) 'Heritage Studies: An Outline', in Marie Louise Stig Sørensen and John Carman (eds.) *Heritage Studies: Methods and Approaches*, London and New York: Routledge, pp. 11–28.

Starn, Randolph (2005) 'A Historian's Brief Guide to New Museum Studies', *The American Historical Review*, vol. 110, no. 1. Online at www.historycooperative. org/journals/ahr/110.1/starn.html. Accessed February 21, 2017.

Stoller, Paul (2017) 'Writing Resistance in the Age of Trump', *The Huffington Post*, January 25. Online at www.huffingtonpost.com/paul-stoller/writing-resistance-in-the_b_14395936.html. Accessed February 21, 2017.

Strathern, Marilyn (2004) 'Working Paper Two: Commons and Borderlands', in *Commons and Borderlands: Working Papers on Interdisciplinarity, Accountability and the Flow of Knowledge*, Wantage, Oxon: Sean Kingston Publishing, pp. 36–50.

Strathern, Marilyn (2016) 'Experimenting With the Contemporary', *Hau: Journal of Ethnographic Theory*, vol. 6, no. 1: 381–6.

Stuever, Hank (2010) 'Glenn Beck's Rally Recap Is One Way to Fill an Hour', *Washington Post*, August 30.

Taylor, Charles (2004) *Modern Social Imaginaries*, Durham: Duke University Press.

Taylor, Kate (2011) 'The Thorny Path to a National Black Museum', *New York Times*, January 22. Online at http://scholarworks.umass.edu/cgi/viewcontent.cgi?article=2129&context=adan. Accessed February 21, 2017.

Third, Amanda (2016) 'The Tactical Researcher: Cultural Studies Research as Pedagogy', in A. Hickey (ed.) *The Pedagogies of Cultural Studies*, New York and London: Routledge, pp. 93–115.

Thomas, Nicholas (2010) 'Commentary: The Museum as Method', *Museum Anthropology*, vol. 33, no. 1: 6–10.

Thrasher, Steven W. (2016) 'The Smithsonian's African American Museum – A Monument to Respectability Politics', *Guardian*, September 17. Online at www. theguardian.com/culture/2016/sep/16/smithsonian-museum-african-american-history-respectability-politics?CMP=share_btn_link. Accessed February 21, 2017.

Tilly, Charles (1978) *From Mobilization to Revolution*, Ann Arbor, MI: Addison-Wesley.

Tilly, Charles (2008) *Contentious Performances*, Cambridge: Cambridge University Press.

Tilly, Charles and Tarrow, Sidney (2007) *Contentious Politics*, Boulder, CO: Paradigm.

Turner, Graeme (2012) *What's Become of Cultural Studies*, London: Sage.

Ulin, Robert (1991) 'Critical Anthropology Twenty Years Later: Modernism and Postmodernism in Anthropology', *Critique of Anthropology*, vol. 11, no. 1: 63–89.

Webb, Jen (2016) 'Ethics and Writing', *The Conversation*, August 4. Online at http://theconversation.com/ethics-and-writing-63399. Accessed February 21, 2017.

Wenger, Etienne (2000) 'Communities of Practice and Social Learning Systems', *Organisation Articles*, vol. 7, no. 2: 225–46.

West Jr., W. Richard (2000) 'A New Idea of Ourselves: The Changing Presentation of the American Indian', in National Museum of the American Indian, Smithsonian Institution (ed.) *The Changing Presentation of the American Indian: Museums and Native Cultures*, Seattle: University of Washington Press, pp. 7–14.

Westcott, Lucy (2016) 'Joe Biden Compares 2016 to 1968', *Newsweek*, December 6. Onlineathttp://europe.newsweek.com/joe-biden-human-rights-award-2016-1968-529273?rm=eu. Accessed February 21, 2017.

Whitehead, Christopher (2007) 'Establishing the Manifesto: Art Histories in the Nineteenth-century Museum', in S.J. Knell, S. MacLeod and S. Watson (eds.) *Museum Revolutions: How Museums Change and Are Changed*, London and New York: Routledge, pp. 45–60.

Whitehead, Christopher (2009) *Museums and the Construction of Disciplines: Art and Archaeology in Nineteenth-Century Britain*, London: Gerald Duckworth & Co. Ltd.

Whitehead, Gudrun D. (2016) 'Reflections on the Icelandic Punk Museum', November 21. Online at https://gudrunwhitehead.wordpress.com/2016/11/21/you-can-do-anythingreflections-on-the-icelandic-punk-museum/. Accessed February 21, 2017.

Wilson, Fred (2010) 'A Change of Heart: Fred Wilson's Impact on Museums', *The Sackler Conference for Arts Education – From the Margins to the Core?* Victoria and Albert Museum, March 24–26. Online (transcript and video) at https://vimeo.com/11838838. Accessed February 21, 2017.

Witcomb, Andrea (2015a) 'Thinking About Others Through Museums and Heritage', in E. Waterton and S. Watson (eds.) *The Palgrave Handbook of Contemporary Heritage Research*, Basingstoke: Palgrave Macmillan, pp. 130–42.

Witcomb, Andrea (2015b) 'Toward a Pedagogy of Feeling: Understanding How Museums Create a Space for Cross-cultural Encounters', in A. Witcomb and K. Message (eds.) *Museum Theory*, Chichester, UK: John Wiley & Sons Ltd., pp. 321–44.

Index

Page numbers in italics indicate figures and page numbers with 'n' indicate notes.

modernity 14n7

moral fear: conservative campaign of 41; and polarized thinking 24–5

Morphy, Howard 15n14, 86n12

Morrison, Toni 31

Murawska-Muthesius, Katarzyna 52

Murawski, Mike 31

Musée du quai Branly 78

museology, new *see* new museology

'Museology as Cultural Studies' (Gable) 79

museum-like events 4, 28, 84

Museum of Impact 96n9

Museum Revolutions (Knell, MacLeod and Watson) 65, 71–3, 76–7, 79

museums: and academic disciplines 9; and activism 27–8, 30–1, 51; authority of 25; as boundary sites 81–2; and campaigns of resistance 26; community-based 37; conflicting missions of 72; as contact zones 77; as contested sites 72; creative resistance of 25; and crisis 26, 44–5, 54; criticism of 26, 31; defining 28; and engagement 82; ethnographic 86n12; and government agendas 52; as ideas 46–8; influence of 27; and language of opposition 71; political nature of 52, 82, 94; and politics 95; politics of representation in 82; protests against 96n4; and the public sphere 42; and radical history 59n11; redefining 81–3; relational 10, 86n12; as safe/unsafe places 42–4, 58n7; self-reflection of 37; as sites of public consciousness 36; and social justice 30–1, 36–7, 59n11, 94; and social/political change 14n9, 26, 31, 38, 45, 51–2, 72, 82–3; and social worlds 9; and spectacle 94; and symbolism 28; transformation in 78; and understanding contemporary life 82; and writing 47

Museums and Racism (Message) 96n10

Museums and Social Activism (Message) 91, 96n10

museum scholarship *see* writing about museums

Museum Social Action Project 96n9

#museumsrespondtoferguson 14n9

museum studies: activist writing in 76; as a boundary discipline 2, 76, 78–9; and community collaboration 37; critical tradition in 54; critical writing in 14n10; and critique 6–7, 31–2, 37, 44, 47, 50–1, 53, 57, 57n1, 91–2, 95; cultural and critical influences on 49; as cultural studies 79; dialectical contemporary in 82; and disciplinary crisis 44; and disciplinary stagnation 36; and engagement 82; interdisciplinarity 78, 80; methodology of 10–11, 13n5; oppositional words in 66; reflective 77–8; reflexive 77–8; and social justice 50–1, 53, 73; and social protest 2; traditional 10; transformation in 79

museum work, politically engaged 4–6

museum writing *see* writing about museums

National Mall *1*, 4, 7, *17*, 28, *35*, 84, 91, 94

National Museum of African American History and Culture 4–5, 22, 33n5, 58n6, 59n11, 89, 96n9

National Museum of American History 19, 21, 96n9

National Museum of Australia 94

National Museum of the American Indian 22, 26, 58n6, 59n11, 78, 94

national museums: and activism 21; creation of 22; inclusion in 58n6; and political reform 37

new museology 76–9

Nixon, Richard 19

'Normalcy, Never Again' (King) 55

Obama, Barack: approach to lobbying by 20; on crisis 55–6; encouragement of activism by 21, 23; inclusive rhetoric of 18; and mobilization of the center 19; and optimism 21–2, 29–30, 56; support for 22

Occupy Archives 59n11

Occupy Movement 18, 21, 30–1, 41, 60n16, 89, 96n2, 96n4

Occupy Museums 59n11

October 64–5, 85n2, 87n14

opposition: and activism 40–3, 56; co-opting of 19; and crisis 57; and critique 65; direct tactics of 23, 29–30; embodied 12; language

Taylor & Francis eBooks

Helping you to choose the right eBooks for your Library

Add Routledge titles to your library's digital collection today. Taylor and Francis ebooks contains over 50,000 titles in the Humanities, Social Sciences, Behavioural Sciences, Built Environment and Law.

Choose from a range of subject packages or create your own!

Benefits for you

» Free MARC records
» COUNTER-compliant usage statistics
» Flexible purchase and pricing options
» All titles DRM-free.

REQUEST YOUR **FREE** INSTITUTIONAL TRIAL TODAY | **Free Trials Available** We offer free trials to qualifying academic, corporate and government customers.

Benefits for your user

» Off-site, anytime access via Athens or referring URL
» Print or copy pages or chapters
» Full content search
» Bookmark, highlight and annotate text
» Access to thousands of pages of quality research at the click of a button.

eCollections – Choose from over 30 subject eCollections, including:

Archaeology	Language Learning
Architecture	Law
Asian Studies	Literature
Business & Management	Media & Communication
Classical Studies	Middle East Studies
Construction	Music
Creative & Media Arts	Philosophy
Criminology & Criminal Justice	Planning
Economics	Politics
Education	Psychology & Mental Health
Energy	Religion
Engineering	Security
English Language & Linguistics	Social Work
Environment & Sustainability	Sociology
Geography	Sport
Health Studies	Theatre & Performance
History	Tourism, Hospitality & Events

For more information, pricing enquiries or to order a free trial, please contact your local sales team: www.tandfebooks.com/page/sales

 Routledge
Taylor & Francis Group | The home of Routledge books

www.tandfebooks.com